Narcocapitalism

Theory Redux

Series editor: Laurent de Sutter

Published Titles
Alfie Bown, *The Playstation Dreamworld*
Laurent de Sutter, *Narcocapitalism:*
Life in the Age of Anaesthesia
Roberto Esposito, *Persons and Things*
Graham Harman, *Immaterialism: Objects and*
Social Theory
Srećko Horvat, *The Radicality of Love*
Dominic Pettman, *Infinite Distraction:*
Paying Attention to Social Media
Nick Srnicek, *Platform Capitalism*

Narcocapitalism
Life in the Age of Anaesthesia

Laurent de Sutter

Translated by Barnaby Norman

polity

First published in 2018 by Polity Press

Polity Press
65 Bridge Street
Cambridge CB2 1UR, UK

Polity Press
101 Station Landing, Suite 300
Medford, MA 02155, USA

ISBN-13: 978-1-5095-0683-5
ISBN-13: 978-1-5095-0684-2 (paperback)

A catalogue record for this book is available from the British Library.

Typeset in 12.5 on 15 pt Adobe Garamond by
Servis Filmsetting Ltd, Stockport, Cheshire
Printed and bound in Great Britain by Clays Ltd, St Ives PLC

The publisher has used its best endeavours to ensure that the URLs for external
websites referred to in this book are correct and active at the time of going to press.
However, the publisher has no responsibility for the websites and can make no
guarantee that a site will remain live or that the content is or will remain appropriate.

Every effort has been made to trace all copyright holders, but if any have been
inadvertently overlooked the publisher will be pleased to include any necessary credits
in any subsequent reprint or edition.

For further information on Polity, visit our website: politybooks.com

'It's all about chemicals.'

Andy Warhol

Contents

Thanks   *page* viii

Prologue: Goin' Down   1
1 Welcome to Prozacland   4
2 Narcocapitalism Unlimited   24
3 Day Without End   45
4 Swallowing the Pill   66
5 The Politics of Overexcitement   87
Epilogue: Gettin' Up   108

Notes   111

Thanks

Sara Amari, Franco Berardi, Pascal Chabot, Ewen Chardronnet, Gilles Collard, Neil de Cort, Nicholas Deschamps, Marguerite Ferry, Peter Goodrich, Line Hjorth, Geraldine Jacques, Elliott Karstadt, Monique Labrune, Louise Lame, Aude Lancelin, Camille Louis, Sophie Marinopoulos, Lilya Aït Menguellet, Barnaby Norman, George Owers, Bernard Stiegler, John Thompson, Henri Trubert, Paul Young, and Marion Zilio.

Prologue

Goin' Down

§o. Patent US4848. On 12 November 1846, Charles Thompson Jackson and William Green Morton, from Boston, filed a patent with the United States Patent Office. It received the number 4848, and, as its introduction noted, concerned the 'improvement of surgical operations'.[1] The improvement in question took the form of a new technique, based on the inhalation of diethyl ether vapours by the patient undergoing the operation, which would produce a state of nervous insensitivity and allow the surgeon to work without causing discernible pain. Even though, as Jackson and Morton acknowledged, this kind of product had been used in the past for various levels of pain reduction, the decision

to use inhalation was still an unprecedented medical move. This was why they were claiming the protection of intellectual property rights for the procedure they had developed; it mattered little that they were only the last link in a long chain of more or less fortuitous discoverers. Indeed, before ether, other forms of inhaled anaesthetic had already been tested – starting with nitrous oxide, used by the English chemist Humphrey Davy in several experiments prior to 1799, twenty years after it had been isolated by Joseph Priestley.[2] And, as early as 1818, Michael Faraday, the inventor of the cage bearing his name, had demonstrated the anaesthetic properties of ether – although it never occurred to him to file a patent for something that seemed to him to be a natural phenomenon.[3] The word 'anaesthetic', moreover, did not yet exist, as any reader of Jackson's and Morton's patent can see; rather than a precisely defined concept, we find vague circumlocutions and general descriptions. It was Oliver Wendell Holmes, the Boston doctor and conversationalist (whose son would become the greatest ever US Supreme Court judge) who, in a letter criticizing his plan to call his invention 'letheon', suggested the word to Morton.[4] The reference to Discord, the goddess of Oblivion, daughter of Eris, seemed dubious to Holmes – after all, with the inhalation of ether, it was less a question of amnesia than insensibility, less a case of returning from the world of the dead than of staying in that of the living. No matter; the US Patent Office gave Jackson and Morton the patent they had asked for – and with this, a new age dawned: the age of anaesthesia.

Chapter 1

Welcome to Prozacland

§1. From symptom to syndrome. When Emil Kraepelin published the sixth edition of his *Lehrbuch der Psychiatrie* in 1899, he had for some time already been a model of scientific success – a model, that is, according to the standards of German science of his day.[1] At the age of thirty, he was made Professor of Psychiatry at the University of Dorpat (today Tartu), in what is now Estonia, quickly becoming head of his department, and then of the hospital attached to it, which he led with strict discipline. From the publication of the first edition of the *Lehrbuch*, in the same year as his habilitation,[2] Kraepelin articulated his programme in a way that left no room for doubt: psychiatry must join the

ranks of the experimental sciences, and aspire to become a branch of medicine. To do this, it would have to give up the metaphysical pre-occupations that had marred the development of psychology, to concentrate on what was most important – understanding the physical causes of mental illnesses.[3] Of course, Kraepelin was not the only one to claim to have brought the field of the medicine of madness into line with the most robust sciences – his teacher, Wilhelm Wundt, himself belonged to what was already a long tra-dition of psychiatrists who had dreamed of hard knowledge.[4] But there was at least one respect in which he set himself apart from his predecessors: his desire to establish a complete clinical picture of the main forms of mental illness, with a view to providing, at last, a system of classification. By turning to the observation of their physical causes, it became possible, he believed, to resolve the difficulties created by the analysis of isolated symptoms, which he grouped together into large families of what he called 'syndromes'.[5] With the publication of each new edition of the *Lehrbuch*, the nosographic designations and the classificatory networks proliferated from his pen, introducing numerous categories destined for great success.

One of the most important amongst these, introduced in the fourth edition of the treatise in 1893, was certainly '*dementia praecox*', which covered every case in which the development of a 'mental weakness' at an inappropriate age was observed. Even though it had been decisively reformulated, it was not, however, this category that made the greatest impression in 1899, but the appearance of a new one, whose sophistication came from the most brutal of short-circuits: 'manic-depressive psychosis'.[6]

*

§2. When being errs. Unexpectedly, for those unfamiliar with his work, Kraepelin did not provide a definition of 'manic-depressive psychosis' (or *manisch-depressiven Irresein* in German), contenting himself with describing the features grouped under this name. These were of either a physical or psychic type, with the latter – present in greater number in Kraepelin's description – including 'sensory disorders' and 'delusional disorders', 'avolition' and 'logorrhea'.[7] Taken in isolation, none of these symptoms would have seemed new; it was their grouping together, and their singular mode of temporal extension, even

across generations, that justified the invention of the 'manic-depressive psychosis' category. That 'melancholic' states could sometimes alternate with 'manic' states bordering on possession was actually something that observers of the human soul had noted since antiquity – it had become a platitude. From Aretaeus of Cappadocia, between the first and fourth centuries CE, to Robert James' *Medicinal Dictionary* in the middle of the eighteenth century, it was understood that, despite their differences, melancholia and mania were two sides of the same illness.[8] In a sense, Kraepelin had been happy simply to synthesize this history into a single nosographic category, which he went on to describe in greater depth than anyone before – anchoring it decisively in the physical domain. For him, the only interest of 'manic-depressive psychosis' was that it gave rise to notable signs – signs whose composition would indicate with certainty the treatment that needed to be prescribed, if indeed there was one. On this point, Kraepelin was hardly an optimist; as he got older, his insistence on the physical dimension of mental illnesses had brought him to defend positions that increasingly leant towards eugenics, and the genetic control of races.[9] Once it had been accepted that physical characteristics were transmitted from generation to generation, it seemed certain to him that mental illnesses, or at least the predisposition to develop them, were also transmitted, with no hope of recovery or redemption. Madness was not an accident that it was possible to survive; it was part of the very being (*Sein*) of the sufferer, whose erring (*Irre*) must continue inevitably, even beyond itself.

*

§3. *What is excitation?* Even though he did not risk a definition of 'manic-depressive psychosis', a disturbing element kept cropping up as Kraepelin went through the symptoms of the illness: 'excitation'. Whatever the symptom described, it was differentiated according to the 'state of excitation' of the patient, which could refer to a physical or psychic agitation, could be positive or negative, and could relate to the 'manic' or the 'depressive' phase. More than the symptom itself, it was its intensification by 'excitation' that should hold the observer's attention, and that, combined with other symptoms of the same order, would allow for the classification of the patient as a victim of 'manic-depressive psychosis'.[10] At one point, as he describes the patient's 'urgent need for activity', he admits it himself: the 'increase in excitability', intensifying excitation as such, should 'perhaps' be considered the 'essential symptom'.[11] The *capacity to be excited*, more than the 'excitation' it was possible to observe, constituted the essential core of the manic-depressive syndrome as Kraepelin understood it – the fact that someone afflicted by the illness could not stand still. The erring of the sufferer's being was neither linear nor planar; it took the form of an oscillation whose movement and amplitude were entirely unpredictable, except in that it was unlikely to stabilize at any point. The manic-depressive was more likely than others to climb aboard the ontological roller coaster, and to abandon being's stable state for a disequilibrium as extreme as it was permanent. In other words: 'manic-depressive psychosis' was being's extreme state, once it had given up on its own constitutive principles – it was extreme *désêtre*, the disorder of being as irresistible temptation. That was what troubled Kraepelin: excitation, for him, meant a rupture in the world order – a regime of intensity challenging the way in which being orientates itself so that it can be qualified as sane. To get rid of the illness, therefore, you would have to attack the capacity to be excited – which is to say, the bodily element that carried being away into extreme regions that no normal human should be allowed to frequent.

*

§4. Enter chloral. Kraepelin's physicalism could have remained a curiosity, relegated to the margins of the history of psychiatry – but, in a few years, it had become the default setting for thinking about mental illnesses in Europe, and then, later, in the United States.[12] This delay is explained by the success that psychoanalysis enjoyed in America at the beginning of the twentieth century – a success based on the opposite hypothesis to Kraepelin's, namely that the milieu of mental illness was the psyche, with language as its epistemological vehicle.[13] If Kraepelin's theory ultimately prevailed across the Atlantic as well, it was because, whatever the hypotheses, there was a point on which everyone agreed – the treatment methods for manic-depressive disorder, or, rather, its principle symptom, excitation. While Kraepelin did not provide any therapeutic advice in his observations on 'manic-depressive psychosis', his clinical prac-

tice, which he passed on to his successors, left no room for doubt on the subject. It must be said that the arsenal available to doctors had recently benefitted from considerable innovations in the world of chemistry – amongst which should be included the invention of a very practical substance: chloral hydrate. Synthesized for the first time in 1831 by the chemist Justus von Liebig, a compatriot of Kraepelin's, chloral hydrate (sometimes erroneously referred to simply as 'chloral') was a substance that any pharmacist could easily produce, but whose effects were formidable. The most interesting of these for psychiatrists was first formally observed in 1869: chloral had properties that were very promising in the field of anaesthetics and sedatives – for the treatment of insomnia, for example.[14] For the director of a psychiatric clinic who had eighty beds to manage, occupied by patients whose principal tendency was towards 'excitation', a substance like this was bound to be of interest for managing his wards. For a long time, chloral hydrate was one of the most common aids available to nurses and doctors grappling with a stubborn patient – demonstrating, that is, what was euphemistically qualified as 'psychomotor agitation'.[15] And for manic-depressive patients, it was even, in line with Kraepelin's pessimistic doctrine, the only treatment they could hope to receive.

*

§5. Powers of deflation. A manic-depressive does not get better; all you can do is try to calm them down – make sure, that is, that the excitation affecting them is reduced to nothing, in favour of an enforced but harmless stability. In other words, with someone suffering from 'manic-depressive psychosis', you can only hope to control the manic element – including what remains of it during a depressive phase. *The only good manic-depressive is a depressive* – separated from the uncontrollable half of their syndrome, the part that justifies their clinical confinement, with the understanding that the care given is limited to the policing of restless bodies. From the moment it was used predominantly to deaden excitation, chloral hydrate's success was assured: if manic excitation was also bodily hyperesthesia, it made sense to remove every sensation that might lead to it. The dynamic of excitation was a dynamic of affection: 'psychomotor agitation' was produced when the sufferer's being was overrun by sensa-

tions and emotions, forcing them off the rails and into the wilds. This is even what the word 'excitation' means: being led outside oneself, being flung out beyond the limits of one's being, being taken by an outside that is beyond the sufferer's control – *to be excited is to experience not being oneself.*[16] 'Manic-depressive psychosis' meant a kind of disontologization: it was how what affects being separated it from itself, in favour of a play of unpredictable forces which threatened to affect other individuals in turn. To fight it, therefore, you had to be able to reinstate being within its limits, to muffle the call of the outside to which it sought to respond, deafening it to what would otherwise lead it to an experience of excess – to an experience that it was assumed was too difficult for it. The sweet anaesthesia afforded by chloral hydrate could fulfil these requirements; where being had inflated out of all proportion, it could bring about its radical deflation through the withdrawal of the affective energies feeding its inflation. Useless sensations were silenced, so that all that was left was a kind of continuous, vaporous and weakened bassline, whose rhythm taught the erring being that the only stroll it could take was around the grounds.

*

§6. A feeling of detachment. But it was not chloral hydrate that ensured the supremacy of Kraepelin's ideas in the field of 'manic-depressive psychosis' – another, even better, invention was needed before the United States would yield to his vision of the illness. This invention was the synthesis of chlorpromazine by Paul Charpentier, a chemist at Rhône-Poulenc researching the effects of histamine, the molecule responsible for many allergic reactions in humans.[17] Noticing that antihistamines had powerful effects on the central nervous system, he began to experiment with different formulas by which some of these could be exploited – including effects of anaesthesia and sedation. On 11 December 1950, he named the latest formula to come from his test tubes 'chlorpromazine', without yet knowing if it would have the slightest use – but hoping that it would have some effectiveness in psychiatry.[18] Tests conducted on a batch of laboratory rats, which suddenly became disinterested in everything after having absorbed the substance, confirmed this almost immediately: as well as anaesthesia and sedation, chlorpromazine brought on *something*

else. This something was articulated by a friend
of the doctor Henri Laborit, who had been following the research underway at Rhône-Poulenc,
when she stated that taking chlorpromazine
produced in her a 'feeling of detachment'.[19]
Several years of further research were necessary
to make sure – but the conclusion was unavoid-
able: acting as a depressant on the central nervous
system, chlorpromazine worked wonders in psy-
chotic patients. Marketed in the United States
in 1955 by Smith, Kline & French as Thorazine,
it immediately became the medicine of choice
in asylums all over the country, opening a new
age in the treatment of mental illness – even if
the word 'treatment' is hardly appropriate.[20] By
way of treatment, chlorpromazine essentially
transformed the person taking it into a passive
spectator of their own mental state, incapable of
feeling that they had been affected by the emotions passing through them. It was no longer a
question of anaesthesia in the surgical sense of the
term, but of a much more profound operation
– anaesthesia in the sense of the ablation of the
relationship between a subject and their sensations, and the elimination of their enjoyment.

*

§7. Enjoying nothing. Just like chloral hydrate, the aim of chlorpromazine was not to cure its users; the only anticipated effect was a levelling-out of the agitation endured by the patient – except that the agitation in question here was as much affective as motor.[21] Overnight, the molecule's success led to a complete shift in American psychiatric thinking, which came around to the idea that the question of mental illnesses could not be settled unless their physical dimension was considered. Before being a sickness of the mind, mental illness was a disorder of the nervous system – and, if you couldn't act on its causes, it was at least now possible to eliminate its most undesirable consequences, both for the patients and for those around them.[22] That this elimination involved putting the concerned party into a new state, where suffering was replaced by indifference, seemed a price worth paying for what appeared to be the soul's return to a form of peace. For individuals afflicted by 'manic-depressive psychosis', or what we now call 'bipolar disorder', this implied a scenario that was very close to that desired by Kraepelin and

the doctors following him.[23] Thanks to chlorpromazine, and all the molecules created in its
wake, the mania could be brought under control,
and the major inconveniences associated with
depression made harmless – in such a way that
it became possible to enjoy yourself a little. In
truth, there was a paradox: when you were on
chlorpromazine, the only thing it was possible
to enjoy was the fact that there was nothing to
enjoy; the only pleasure was the absence of pleasure, a sort of degree zero of the affective life. Of
course, you could argue that the anaesthesia was
not total, since the medication's users at least
perceived that they perceived nothing; but this
kind of meta-perception of the perceptions nonetheless indicated the extent to which they had
been deprived of something. From Kraepelin's
perspective, this something could only be the
outside in which the patient risked losing their
being; for those who looked carefully, it was an
essential dimension of being itself – supposing
the concept has any meaning – that had been
excised. Where chloral hydrate enabled the control of being's explosion, chlorpromazine made
the control of its implosion – its collapse in the
middle of itself – conceivable.

*

§8. A brief defence of stability. The question of depression had always been a question of ontology; it had always been connected to the way in which being was disposed – and to the way in which this disposition was, or was not, considered desirable, according to rules, norms or ideas whose origins remained mysterious.[24] Kraepelin had his, haunted by considerations of racial purity, and the promotors of antidepressants, coming after Rhône-Poulenc or Smith, Kline & French, nurtured theirs – or tried to satisfy those they identified with. We are always dealing with conceptions resonating with those of the epoch; we are not dealing with conceptions differing significantly from those of what we might crudely call the 'ideology' of the time. It was clear for Kraepelin, as it was for the champions of chlorpromazine, that the most important thing was stability: the most important concern, which should obsess every psychiatrist, was to put a stop to erring – to excitation's uncontrolled oscillations. Being's necessity had to be affirmed, and this affirmation accompanied by a defence of everything that kept it in its limits, in the

double sense of confinement and permanence – a defence, that is, of what prevented it from taking off in all directions. Contrary to what we might at first think, affirming being's necessity was not at all a neutral thesis – it even recalled one of metaphysics' most ancient vocations: namely, the policing of beings. To consider being as a category whose stability could offer guarantees against the internal and external forces likely to break up individuals was to assign a powerful horizon of normality to patients. *You had to be* – you had to deny yourself indulgence in the vague, floaty, scattered states that characterize so many mental illnesses, which may have offered something of benefit to their sufferers, however strange and fleeting. You had to settle down in being, so that you could also settle down in everything it underpinned, the most obvious being that great fragmentary body whose potential instability was a source of so many fears amongst stronger spirits, and which a nascent science had called 'society'. Being was not only the key to individual health; it also held out the possibility of protecting the social body itself from the defects afflicting those who constituted it.

*

§9. Side effects. An indication of how the 'treatment' of patients was based on concerns that exceeded them, could be found in the side effects of the medications they were prescribed – and the light touch of the law in this area.[25] While chloral hydrate is now amongst the most highly regulated substances on Earth, antidepressants enjoy a remarkable degree of tolerance from the authorities, even though they can have very harmful consequences. The range is very broad, and includes muscular spasms, a slowing of cognitive activity, a paradoxical risk of dependency, Parkinson-type symptoms, bouts of akathisia, and even a fatal disruption to the nervous system. But most revealing, in terms of the way in which neuroleptic antidepressants like chlorpromazine work, is the fact that most users end up suffering from anhedonia and sexual impotence.[26] Not only can the detachment effect make it impossible to feel pleasure physically, but this impossibility can manifest itself in a total ablation of sexual desire – as being's driving force. That an individual might no longer feel or desire anything seemingly poses no problem for doctors or public

authorities (or pharmaceutical companies); it is even accepted that this is the ultimate meaning of the phrase 'getting better'. 'Getting better' is not getting anywhere at all – it is existing only in the negative mode of a being whose stability badly conceals the emptiness, as well as the suffering of not suffering, or of feeling that you do not feel your suffering, in an inescapable downward spiral. That the being on which the chemistry of 'manic-depressive psychosis' bases its experiments is a being characterized by asthenia and impotence, by the anaesthesia of sensation or desire, should long ago have alerted us to the contradictions of this 'getting better'. If they do not seem to bother any of the protagonists in the psycho-political theatre of contemporary depression, this is, no doubt, because in truth no one would have it any other way – they would not want finally to cure it, for example. Still today, chlorpromazine features on the list of 'essential medications' that has been published every other year since 1977 by the World Health Organization (WHO) – in the chapter on 'mental and behavioral disorders'.[27]

*

§10. After biopolitics. When the first edition of the *Diagnostic and Statistical Manual of Mental Disorders* (or *DSM*) was published in 1952, based on a model provided by a classificatory schema suggested by the American army during World War II, it was already well furnished. The 130 pages identified 106 mental disorders, amongst which several were grouped under the heading 'Personality disorder', to be differentiated from the more clinical 'neurosis'. Amongst these 'disorders', it was still possible to find homosexuality, which – implying at the time a traumatic parent–child relationship – was considered a 'sociopathic' practice.[28] It was not until the third edition of the *DSM*, in 1980, however, that what had been clear to the discerning reader was explicitly set out by the committee in charge of revising the manual – now presented as an aid to public regulation. This revision, undertaken by a committee chaired by the psychiatrist Robert Spitzer, did not hide the fact that the method used to systematize the manual, and harmonize it with international practices, was based on a particular understanding of mental illness. This understanding was designated 'neo-Kraepelinian', since it had now been established that the best way to deal with

'mental disorders' was to connect each pathology with a given syndrome.[29] This was the ultimate endorsement for Kraepelin's ideas: once the authors of the *DSM* had declared their faith in them, world psychiatry had to follow – just as it had to conform to their regulatory concerns. The classificatory system of 'mental disorders' had become an instrument of population management, whose principal concern was to identify what had previously been upbraided in homosexuality. The diagnosis of mental illness was no longer a diagnosis directed towards the sufferer, but a serious accusation, entailing that the 'disorder' in question should be subject to the sustained attention of public authorities – because you had to stop it from spreading. Thanks to this, the old biopolitics of the body could be confined to governmental obscurity; psychopolitics had come onto the world stage, and it was going nowhere.[30]

Chapter 2

Narcocapitalism Unlimited

§11. Act locally, think globally. In the years following Jackson and Morton's patenting of their
system for anaesthetizing through the inhalation of diethyl ether, just about everyone became
interested in the possibilities opened by the
invention of narcosis – even if only to criticize.[1]
Being able to plunge individuals into a sleep that
nothing, even the worst suffering, could disturb,
promised considerable financial gain and a guaranteed scientific career to whoever was able to
provide the best version. Countless substances
were accordingly tested, until a new discovery silenced those who still considered general
anaesthesia a dangerous technique – along with
other techniques requiring the greatest meticu-

lousness. In 1860, the Austrian chemist Albert Niemann managed to isolate the main active ingredient in the coca leaves brought back to Vienna by Carl Scherzer, the great contemporary adventurer, and concluded that it possessed completely unprecedented anaesthetic properties.[2] Where diethyl ether plunged the person who had inhaled it into a state of total unconsciousness, cocaine produced a lasting localized effect – a perfect, but circumscribed, insensitivity at the place of application or injection. The news provoked extraordinary enthusiasm, first with laryngologists who started using it in 1877, twelve years after cocaine's alkaloid nature had been put beyond doubt by Niemann's successor, Wilhelm Lossen.[3] In the field of ophthalmology, the news was also greeted as a benediction, apparent in the reception the first paper on the subject enjoyed during the annual conference of the German Society of Ophthalmology in Heidelberg in 1884. Karl Koller, a 26-year-old scientist, reported on the effectiveness of injecting cocaine for anaesthetizing the cornea and the conjunctiva, and on how this meant that it was possible to imagine other applications in the field of painful ocular complaints.[4] But Koller was modest: despite the success of his experiments, he made a point of underscoring their debt to the intuitions of a Viennese colleague attached to the same hospital, who had, he said, established a 'complete history of cocaine'.[5] This colleague had not yet made much of an impression, even though he had already published an article on the subject, and had himself begun research, which he had had to suspend, on the possible ophthalmological uses of cocaine. His name was: Sigmund Freud.

*

§12. 'Über Coca'. It was in July 1884 that Freud, who was just two years older than Koller, published in *Centralblatt für die gesammte Therapie* the results of his research into the therapeutic use of cocaine, based on experiments undertaken on his own person.[6] After a few generalities on the history of the coca plant, its use by Andean peoples and the discovery of the active ingredients it contained, the young psychiatrist began by reviewing the state of medical knowledge on the subject.[7] In truth, it was more of a panegyric than a review, such was Freud's insistence on the surprising nature of the observations of his predecessors, all of whom testified to the many virtues that could be associated with the consumption of coca. For Freud, there was no doubt that cocaine was, above all, promising – and that was what his experiments were meant to demonstrate definitively to those who continued to venture doubts.[8] For two months, he had submitted himself to the regular ingestion of 0.05 grams of *cocainum muriaticum*, diluted at 1 per cent in a water solution, and had recorded the principal physiological and psychological results. His verdict was definitive: cocaine represented a marvellous stimulant, from which no unpleasant short- or medium-term side effects should be expected – enabling sustained intellectual or physical tasks to be accomplished effortlessly and without tiring. With respect to patients, ingesting cocaine was to be recommended for stomach trouble, cachexia, asthma, detoxification from alcoholism and morphine addiction – not to mention its aphrodisiac and anaesthetic applications.[9] But the most obvious use to acknowledge was still that it offered a means of protection for sufferers of 'those functional states comprised under the name *neurasthenia*', or the weakening of nervous strength.[10] In the struggle with the depression of nervous activity, cocaine could

intervene as a suppressor, producing an insensitivity to 'depressing elements', and distancing the
subject from their bodily organs, the source of
this depression.[11] Cocaine not only could act as a
bodily anaesthetic, but also functioned as a nervous anaesthetic – thanks to which the nervous
system supporting the psyche could be consigned
to oblivion.

*

§13. Meanwhile in Darmstadt. As it happens,
Freud was not using just any old cocaine; as he
mentions in a note in his article 'Über Coca',
it was 'chlorohydric cocaine prepared by Merck
in Darmstadt' – the best in the world.[12] In fact,
since the family pharmacy had been taken over
by Emanuel Merck in 1817, it had transformed
itself into a veritable industry, specializing in the
production of all kinds of alkaloids serving as the
basis for numerous medical preparations. Most
famous amongst them was a commercial version
of the active agent in poppies, which had been isolated by another pharmacist, Friedrich Sertürner,
between 1803 and 1805, and which Joseph-Louis
Gay-Lussac had called 'morphine'; Merck had
been selling it in its own name since 1827.[13] As

for cocaine, the company started synthesizing it barely two years after Niemann had discovered it – although for a long time this was in minuscule quantities (less than 50 grams per year at the end of the 1870s). Nevertheless, Merck's expertise in the synthesis of alkaloids, and the exceptional quality of the products coming out of its laboratories, made it the partner of choice for anyone researching in this area. Freud was not alone in approaching Merck for his cocaine supply; Koller also got what he needed for his experiments from the Darmstadt company – like Theodor Aschenbrandt, who was interested in its military applications.[14] The curiosity for its product shown by these researchers, along with the general tenor of their research, ultimately aroused the company's interest in what it had thought of as a niche product with minimal commercial potential. Following the publication of his article, it sponsored a study by Freud on another alkaloid present in coca leaves, whose structure is close to that of cocaine: ecgonine – but no convincing results came of it.[15] This did not stop Merck from initiating an awareness-raising campaign amongst doctors on the properties of its product, in the form of brochures sent to their surgeries extolling its effectiveness in the treatment of morphine addiction. Demand seems to have followed, since, from a production of 1.41 kilograms in 1883, the factory went on to produce 30 kilograms in 1885 – with the unit price doubling, then quadrupling, during the same period.[16]

*

§14. Capitalism's Merck moment. In the years following Merck's promotional campaign, the substance's success was such that several competitors, like Boehringer and Knoll, also entered the market, making Germany a world leader in cocaine production. At the beginning of the 1920s, it was estimated that nearly all the Peruvian coca production passed through Hamburg, and that the extracted cocaine constituted 80 per cent of world trade in the sector – a trade that was extraordinarily profitable.[17] While the clauses of the Treaty of Versailles forced the German authorities to conform to the rules of the International Opium Convention, this only affected Merck and its colleagues incidentally; by the middle of the 1930s, everything was back to normal. Merck took its place at the head of

two business cartels whose aim was to divide up the global narcotics market, while strengthening links between representatives of public authorities – one of which was called the 'convention on cocaine'.[18] Contrary to what one might imagine, the Nazis coming to power, and the implementation of the systematic purification of the drug-addicted population, did not change this situation very much; in certain respects, it even helped to accentuate it. From one perspective, the word 'cocaine' had become synonymous with degeneration – but the molecules only had to be called something else, and given a medical justification, and what had become a dangerous drug would start to look like an essential product.[19] Furthermore, once World War II had broken out, some of these substances played a decisive role in the military victories of the Wehrmacht, whose soldiers, under the orders of military doctors, consumed amphetamine derivatives in huge quantities. And the cocaine-producing enterprises quickly discovered interesting alternatives, like oxycodone, a derivative of a poppy alkaloid, whose properties as an alternative to morphine were exploited by Merck from 1928. Amongst Merck's best clients, incidentally, was

Theodor Morell, Adolf Hitler's personal doctor, who prescribed astounding quantities of products from the company catalogue – from glucose to oxycodone.[20] For half a century, even though the dangers associated with the consumption of opium and coca derivatives were becoming increasingly clear, German industrial capitalism enjoyed one of its greatest periods of euphoria.

*

§15. A page of advertising. We should add, however, that it was not alone; while Koller, Freud and Aschebrandt were being seduced by Merck's products, another aspect of capitalism's development was finding a valuable ally in cocaine. In 1863, having got wind of Niemann's discovery, and having obtained the works of the Italian doctor Paolo Mantegazza (which formed the basis of Freud's research), Angelo Mariani, a Corsican pharmacist living in Paris, launched a new product onto the market.[21] It claimed to be a 'tonic wine', and consisted of an infusion of coca leaves in a Bordeaux wine – an infusion that released the alkaloids contained in the leaves, amongst which, of course, was the 'stimulant' cocaine.[22] Mariani was not the first to market

this kind of beverage, but he was, however, a pioneer in the use of a device that would ensure its success, and make 'Mariani Wine' one of the most famous and highly praised drinks of the end of the nineteenth century. In an epoch flooded with charlatans offering the public variously adulterated products by way of 'adverts' featured in newspapers, you needed to come up with a way of advertising that would stand out from your competitors'. Mariani ensured that the biggest celebrities of the day, including several popes and heads of state, received cases of his wine as a gift, in the hope of a return compliment that he could use at a later date to promote his product. The strategy worked so well that he was able to collect the declarations of his illustrious patrons into albums illustrated by the greatest artists of the day, which he followed up with spin-off products and events to make sure that his wine was continually being talked about.[23] Like Merck's success, Mariani's immediately attracted many competitors – but the indisputable quality of the product, along with the Corsican's irresistible marketing technique, consigned more or less all of them to oblivion. The gradual adoption of laws targeting the consumption of alcohol in the

United States, one of the most important markets for the producers of 'tonic wine', was not helpful; Mariani himself was affected by them – even if his coca drink continued to be sold until 1910.[24] Some, however, were able to get around the prohibitions to which Mariani and his competitors succumbed; the most important was a certain John Pemberton, producer of a 'French Wine Coca' in Atlanta, who ended up substituting a syrup for the wine – and marketing it as 'Coca-Cola'.[25]

*

§16. The Coke side of life. Like 'Mariani Wine', the Coca-Cola launched by Pemberton in May 1886 contained the equivalent of 10 grams of cocaine per liter, and was purported to possess the same stimulating and tonic properties – it only lacked alcohol.[26] Rather than sell it as a medication, the pharmacist decided to make it a 'refreshing drink' that could be bought in grocery stores; it was not as successful as hoped, and Pemberton sold his invention, before dying from the consequences of his morphine addiction.[27] If the product was subsequently to enjoy the success we know, this was thanks to the commercial genius

of Asa Candler, the businessman who bought Coca-Cola's name and formula from Pemberton, and decided on the now-iconic bottle shape in 1915. In the meantime, in 1903, Coca-Cola had dropped the cocaine, while continuing to include in its formula an infusion of coca leaves – which it still does today, thanks to a bespoke exception, appearing in Article 27 of the United Nations' Single Convention on Narcotic Drugs of 1961. This exception, authorizing The Coca-Cola Company to import coca leaves from Bolivia for its own use, enjoyed the support of Harry J. Anslinger, one of the most equivocal personalities in the history of the Unites States' war on drugs.[28] As the first chief of the Federal Bureau of Narcotics, he never stopped painting drugs, especially marijuana, in the worst light possible, resorting to the most brazen disinformation manoeuvres – with the support of the William Randolph Hearst newspapers and the DuPont de Nemours group. Scandals created out of nothing, the association of drug consumption with 'dangerous' (meaning non-white) communities, etc., made up the arsenal that Anslinger used to justify his work – and to claim more credit for his department. His methods may finally have put an end to his career, but President Kennedy still appointed him, before his retirement, as the United States representative to the United Nations' Commission on Narcotic Drugs.[29] It was no small paradox that this man from the war on drugs was also the man through whom one of the largest businesses to benefit from coca culture could continue to get its raw materials – while excluding all competition. If you really think about it, however, this paradox was totally logical: it involved an addiction like any other.

*

§17. Introduction to economic pharmacology. From Merck to Coca-Cola, by way of Mariani and his imitators, at the beginning of the development of industrial capitalism, cocaine played a role similar to the one it was meant to play for its consumers: the role of the most powerful stimulant. It was thanks to it (and certain related products) that the modern pharmaceutical industry managed to get off the ground, and that the market for countering neurasthenia became so profitable that it wiped out the small-time charlatans. Clearly, this kind of development could not take place without producing embarrassing grey areas – and, in

fact, cocaine is always to be found where modern capitalism is most susceptible to suspicions of corruption, namely in its relationship with public authorities. Whether we are talking about the role played by narcotic substances during World War II (and, more broadly, during the whole history of twentieth-century warfare), or about how they are hidden, under other names, in the pharmacopeia during peacetime, the dark side of modernity is unthinkable without them. Cocaine's gradual relegation to the margins of illegality changed nothing: still today, the world economy only sustains itself on the money that circulates in it from the extraction, transformation and trade in the alkaloid. At the time of the subprime crisis in 2007, it was the profits from cocaine trafficking that enabled the banks, whose gambling had put them in a difficult position, to survive while they waited for the state to put its hand in its pocket and get them out of a fix. For a few months, when traditional investors were withdrawing their cash from the banks, only drug dealers carried on pumping liquidity into the system – which they needed to give their cash a legal appearance.[30] Just as industrial capitalism had been made possible by cocaine, it was to cocaine that it delegated the task of saving it from itself, having become intoxicated by its own power following the turn to financialization – born, by another paradox, in the same period as the 'war on drugs'. This can only remind us of the sales arguments put forward by Merck as the Darmstadt company tried to persuade European doctors that cocaine's primary aim was the treatment of morphine addiction – which, *from a certain perspective*, was not false.[31] In both instances, it is a matter of expecting a poison to become its own remedy.

*

§18. Let it go, let it go. Freud believed his research conclusions were irrefutable: cocaine was a substance whose principal effect was to make an activity possible that was not possible without it – by performing a kind of distancing of what was preventing it. In other words, *cocaine was an efficacy operator*: when an individual was suffering from difficulties associated with a depressive state, or from physical disturbances, the substance allowed this suffering to be discounted. It was in this sense that it could be called a 'stimulant' (or, as with Mariani Wine, a 'tonic'): it pushed

into action – an action that it both stimulated and made possible through the removal of anything that resisted this stimulation. 'Resistance' meant anything associated with the brake that matter is always liable to deploy – or, rather: the brake that matter, by its very nature and density, cannot help constituting, like the body and its organs. Thanks to cocaine, the site of action was displaced from the motor body to pure will, to the exercise of mental faculties detached from any contingency except their own power, as though it were possible that matter was nothing but their servant. When Freud argued that cocaine enabled the recreation of 'excitement' where it seemed to have vanished, this is doubtless what he meant: that the product he was ordering for a fortune from Merck liberated him from everything that was preventing him from acting – namely, himself. The most important thing, in any case, was not the ablation phenomenon he observed, but the fact that this led to a mobilization: cocaine made you mobile, active, effective again; it enabled the accomplishment of the most arduous and urgent tasks without the least effort. In short, cocaine was the brain's fuel – it is what enabled the brain to be itself, while the rest of the self (the body) was shut away in the cupboard, so that it could give itself over unreservedly to the enjoyment of its own operation. Freud did not go so far as to say that taking cocaine made him more intelligent or perspicacious; he had not yet attained the megalomaniac stage of cocaine addiction – but there was nonetheless a touch of that in his writings on the subject. It was in his private correspondence with his fiancée Martha that he gave free rein to the lyric description of what cocaine made him do at society dinners – but his scientific articles were no less laudatory.[32]

*

§19. The same stuff as dreams. That cocaine constituted a principle of subjective efficacy, and that this principle took the form of a kind of abstraction with respect to matter and to its constraining nature, was the main lesson to be found in the texts that Freud dedicated to the substance. But his relationship with Merck, as well as the way in which the company served as a metonym for the workings of industrial capitalism, should make us wonder if there wasn't more to it. With cocaine, it was a question of a kind of logic of detachment – a kind of process of general dematerialization,

affecting every dimension of reality, whether of a subject or of a social universe. Cocaine is the principle of efficacy of a floating world – a world in which nothing counts any more, except the free deployment of powers authorized by the forgetting of anything that could constrain them, in any sphere. This, moreover, is what the history of the cocaine trade ended up revealing: that there was no limit or rule that could oppose it – or, if there was, you might just as well ignore it, now that none could hold up. When, in a press conference in 1971, Richard Nixon launched his 'war on drugs', he knew full well that it was a hopeless war, since every new attempt to contain the cocaine trade would see it slip farther away.[33] This, indeed, may have been his goal: to ensure that a kind of movement of abstract struggle was initiated, which had no existence or consistence except as a pure flux or pure force – the pure gesture of a decision without any relationship to the reality it was supposed to confront. Symptomatically, it was also in 1971 that Nixon decided to suspend the convertibility of the dollar into gold, a decision that put an end both to the Bretton Woods Agreement, which had kept the world economy more or less stable, and to any link between American money and its standard.[34] The global economic system suddenly found itself plunged into a kind of plastic madness, whose first effect was the roll-out of finance, that gigantic machine for producing money without any reference except to its own value. In the same way that the only consequence of the war on drugs was the disappearance of what remained of materiality in the cocaine trade, the end of the Bretton Woods Agreement marked capitalism's entry into the era of its dematerialization.

*

§20. Zero, zero, zero. In the terrifying investigation of the Mafioso workings of the cocaine economy that he published in 2013, Roberto Saviano suggested an even more radical hypothesis – according to which, what only seemed to be a coincidence was in fact a common nature.[35] The role played by the coke trade in the history of industrial development, as well as the model the substance represented in the turn to financialization, should have made us suspect that there was more going on with capitalism than simple amorality. Rather than a system accompanying (and even, largely, supported by) the powder that

fascinated Freud, capitalism should be thought of as being completely innervated by it – in that it constitutes its energy, its substance, its goal and its model. Not only is international finance inseparable from the drug trade, but every-thing indicates that *it is just one single thing* – as though it were impossible to distinguish the two, as Nixon's equivocations already demonstrated. *The only capitalism is cocaine capitalism* – in the same way that cocaine only exists in an economic system appropriate to its volatility, its illegality, its addictiveness and its immateriality, which is to say, an abstract nervous system that has become perfect excitation. Every capitalism is, necessarily, a narcocapitalism – a capitalism that is narcotic through and through, whose excitability is only the manic reverse of the depression it never stops producing, even as it presents itself as its remedy. Of course, this remedy is nothing but a forget-ting – that ablation of organ sensation that Freud highlighted, which ultimately found its ideal form in the anaesthesia practised every day on millions of consumers of antidepressants. And it is no doubt not by chance that most of the anti-depressants on the market share a lot more with cocaine than their synthetic nature and the effect of anaesthesia brought on by their consumption. Rereading Freud, what we were entitled to expect from cocaine was precisely what the anxious inhabitants of the ruins of global capitalism hope to get from the pills that they swallow all day long: to feel nothing – above all not their stomach. Narcocapitalism is the capitalism of narcosis, that enforced sleep into which anaesthetists plunge their patients so as to unburden them from everything that prevents them from being efficient in the current arrangement – which means work, work and more work.

Chapter 3

Day Without End

§21 An end to insomnia. The publication in 1869 of the book that the German chemist Oscar Liebreich had decided to dedicate to a description of the merits of chloral hydrate had an effect that neither he, nor his editor, expected: overnight it made the substance famous.[1] This fame became a little awkward as it quickly spread beyond the restricted circles of specialists in chemistry and medicine, to reach a mainstream always on the lookout for new miracle medicines in the fight against its afflictions. One of the most difficult of these battles was with insomnia: for a long time, the only remedies available to sufferers were diets, bloodletting or potions that had more in common with witches' brews.[2] Actual medications were

limited to various kinds of narcotics extracted from plants – the most famous being laudanum, an opium derivative owing its name to Paracelsus who, in the sixteenth century, was amongst the first to engage in experiments on the medical properties of poppies. The problem with laudanum (as with opium in general) was that it was very powerfully addictive, counting many famous figures amongst its victims, including Samuel Taylor Coleridge and Charles Dickens, Thomas De Quincey and Charles Baudelaire.[3] The discovery of chloral hydrate was a godsend: thanks to it, modern medicine finally had a sedative that it could use to combat insomnia without having to worry about fatal side effects – this, at least, was what they thought for a time. It was used massively in psychiatric hospitals to calm the manic 'excitation' of certain patients, and it was also the drug of choice for all those who suffered from an inability to take advantage of the moments of forgetting that would allow them to fall asleep. As was the case with mental illness, these users of chloral hydrate were seeking a kind of calm – a lessening of nervous excitation, a reduction of 'psychomotor agitation' to its absolute minimum. This was not by chance: for many

observers of nocturnal life, there was a direct connection between insomnia and what Kraepelin
would later call 'manic-depressive psychosis', as
though the former could be considered a symptom of the latter.[4] For a long time, this is what
was thought: for moralists and doctors, melan-
cholics – like women, children and libertines
– had a problem with the night.[5]

*

§22. The price of the night. The good worker
sleeps well – for the simple man who has completed his labours by the book, this represents
a greater reward than his salary; the victims of
insomnia are the others – the slackers, the idle
and the indolent. So runs a stereotype common
in medical circles, whose origins go back to the
dawn of time: sleep is the honest man's rest, and
the torment of those whose existence yields to
impropriety, of whatever kind. For all those who
looked favourably on the development of industrial capitalism, this assessment was something
of a principle: what was needed were individuals
who slept soundly – so that they could get on with
their work unhampered the next day. In *Capital*,
published two years before Liebrich's book on

chloral hydrate, Karl Marx called the process in which sleep played a decisive role the 'reproduction of labor power' – its other parameter, which interested him even more, was salary.[6] The night, and the enforced inactivity that went with it, was the price that capitalists were ready to pay in order to extract sufficient surplus value from those working for them during the day – and it had to be paid by the workers as well. Much more than a simple factor that had to be accommodated, the night became a decisive element in the establishment of the capitalist order; it was responsible for its smooth running – or its disorder. But the question was: what night? As Marx demonstrated in the passage in Volume 1 of *Capital* where he described the struggles associated with determining the duration of the working day, the whole question of the surplus value the capitalist extracted from the labour power he drew on depended on time.[7] For there to be surplus value, a time supplementing the time necessary for the simple reproduction of labour power had to be accounted for; it was this 'extra' time, according to Marx, that became central to what capitalism wrested from the worker.[8] By 'extra' time, we should understand: the time for which the capitalist did not pay – knowing that it had to be precisely calculated, in order to avoid an excess of 'extra' time becoming, through a lack of night, the time of the workers' exhaustion. Even though he said nothing about it in his treatise, the night was the standard by which the value of work was measured – it was that on which capitalism purported to exercise dominion.

*

§23. *Ius nocturnis.* But the encroachment on the night by the forces of order did not have to wait until the middle of the nineteenth century; however far back you go, it has always been presented as a danger for which the only solution was sleep. Throughout the seventeenth century, for example, Italian and German jurists were equally ingenious in the elaboration of what was called '*ius nocturnis*' (the law of the night) – a law whose principal objective was to try to formalize the extent to which the night was a milieu to be feared.[9] To prove this, they turned to the resemblance between the terms *nox* (night) and *noxa* (harm), implying that there was something in the very fact of the night that was harmful or injurious.[10] In general terms, this association led

them to consider it self-evident that carrying out
an objectionable act nocturnally was a punishable
proclivity – or, in any case, that it constituted an
aggravating factor with respect to the act in question. This aggravation may go so far as to justify
the killing of the aggressor, when they benefitted from their victim's vigilance being reduced to
nothing by sleep – or it could allow the automatic
assumption of premeditation.[11] The most curious
thing, however, was not so much the insistence
on the juridical implications of the passage from
day to night, but the way in which this insistence was based on the presentation of the latter
as the site of all danger, from which you should
protect yourself at any price. With the jurists of
ius nocturnis, we are not witnessing the juridical
discovery of the nocturnal milieu, but its establishment as an ecology of harm – an ecology that,
the jurists did not fail to highlight, was full of
monsters.[12] This elevation of the night to the
level of the natural preserve of malevolent spirits
certainly had precedents – but the insistence with
which this almost evil dimension was hammered
home suggested that something else was in play.
And this something else was nothing less than the
invasion of the night by the forces of order – the

increasingly assured desire to turn it into a territory yielding to sovereign power in the same way
as the day, whereas, previously, it had continued
to elude it. For too long, the night had meant a
vague space, where festivity and a certain notion
of rest were protected from the gaze of masters
and proprietors; this obscurity now had to be
conquered.[13]

*

§24. *What enlightenment really is.* Paris was the
first city to decide on the installation of a modern
system of public lighting; in 1667, the new
Lieutenant General of the police, Gabriel Nicolas
de la Reynie, decreed that every part of the street
should be illuminated by a fixed lantern.[14] This
was his first act following his appointment to
his new position by Jean-Baptiste Colbert, and
it inaugurated both modern policing and the
nocturnal administration of the city – as though
the two were in the end the same thing. It is
true that it was initially only a matter of double
wick candles, protected from bad weather by a
simple windbreak – and not a sophisticated grid
of gas streetlights giving off light through a thin
window pane, as in the nineteenth century. But

this did not stop la Reynie celebrating victory over the Parisian night with a medal, struck in 1669, on which the following motto could be read: '*urbis securitas et nitor*' ('the security and probity of the town').[15] La Reynie's idea was indeed to clean the city streets, in every sense of the term – which is to say, get rid of everything that made it an unclean, insalubrious city, that was dangerous and difficult to control, above all when its roads were emptied of people. For him, ensuring the city's security meant ensuring that the night was no longer a stretch of time escaping his authority, and therefore, by extension, the king's; the night too must recognize the full extent of the sovereignty of power. *The citizen had to be seen to sleep* – that, in the end, was the desire la Reynie nurtured; the citizens should shut themselves away in their houses, and the officers of his police should be able to verify this without being fooled by those who lived in the shadows. If the night was to remain a place for rebuilding strength, which made diurnal activities possible, it had to do so in full light – the very light that historians would retrospectively make the herald of the century it illuminated. The Enlightenment was nothing but the introduction of day where, until then, it had been unable to shine its light; its method presented no surprises: Enlightenment was the police plus urban illumination. Before putting an end to political or religious 'obscurantism', you first had to put an end to physical obscurity; this is what la Reynie undertook with a zeal that everyone applauded, and that kept him in post for thirty years, even though he could have been removed at any time.[16]

*

§25. A trip to Webster Hall. Chloral hydrate's success at the end of the nineteenth century could be interpreted as the success of a conception of the night subjected to the law-enforcement idea that saw it as the place for rebuilding strength – and so as the criterion of the moral division between the good and the bad worker. But it goes without saying that this conception could not have avoided generating its contrary, and that the simultaneous invention of night policing and public lighting made other ways of filling the time possible – ways which left a lot to be desired. In 1886, the opening in New York of Webster Hall, the first modern nightclub, indicated the direction in which things were heading:

towards the reinvention of the orgy in the age of electric lighting and the player piano.[17] While the old taverns maintained a relationship with the night that was that of any domestic dwelling, nightclubs saw themselves as beacons across the darkness, without at any time feeling the obligation to abjure. In other words, the appearance of the nightclub signified the appearance of a way of appropriating the nocturnal world which aimed at evading the police – or rather, turning them to its advantage, given that they were supposed to have cleared the darkness of any danger. The reason for the long wait between the time when the first lanterns were installed in the cities and the opening of the first nightclub was that public lighting lacked the intensity and effectiveness that only the transition to electricity could achieve. The use of coal gas, then natural gas, at the beginning of the nineteenth century, had already made urban illumination easier – but it was the general introduction of electricity in the 1880s that completed the conquest of the night, transforming it into a place for life comparable to any other.[18] It was to this life that the nightclub bore witness – a life which, if you looked closely, had the appearance of a slightly contorted simulacrum, seen in the sweating faces of dancers who had drunk a little too much. In the case of Webster Hall, we should add that the faces were often those of workers and militant leftists, who went there to hold meetings, trade-union rallies or fundraisers for cooperatives.[19] Not only was the invention of the nightclub the invention of a modern form of excess, it also implied the invention of a modern form of politics, whose relationship with the existing order was, to say the least, critical.

*

§26. Politics of excitation. For a long time, nocturnal social life had been a private life – one enjoyed by those whose dwellings had reception rooms and gardens to contain the excesses reserved for holders of a pass. The invention of the nightclub represented a kind of proletarian response to the private hoarding of celebration – a way of returning celebration to its public nature, always involving more guests than appeared on the lists drawn up by the lady of the house. The authorities made no mistake here: when they determined what kind of space nightclubs represented, they decided to consider them 'public spaces', which

is to say spaces in which specific rules regarding security and decency should apply.[20] Since the night had been domesticated, new activities should of course be permitted – but on condition that they did not exceed the narrow framework of what the existing order was prepared to accept; if the orgy was to be permitted, it had to be contained. We know that the first nightclubs were meeting places for proletarian workers – this desire to limit any excesses that might occur in the clubs was also a desire to limit the possible reasons for these excesses. Along with those produced by alcohol, dance and the vagaries of human relations, we should include those implying a political form of excitation – the contamination of minds by the forces of scandal, and their transformation into demands for social justice. The nightclub, as a place of communal excess, represented an environment that was conducive to the circulation of all kinds of affects, which could just as well produce a brawl over a sexual escapade or lay the foundations of a general strike. This was part and parcel of the new dangers created by the policing of the night: while it was impossible to raise further the spectre of demons and spirits hostile to the good sleepers, it was perfectly possible to make them think that they had materialized in new bodies. These bodies constituted what the demographer Louis Chevalier in 1958 termed the 'dangerous classes' – who were also, precisely, the 'labouring classes': a labour force – in the service of a capitalist proprietor – from whom revenue was extracted.[21] 'The security and probity' of the city, of which La Reynie boasted, had not removed the need for nocturnal monsters; the club became their zoo.

*

§27. Here is to Mickey Finn. The inversion of the restorative night into a disturbing night is illustrated by another paradoxical oddity, brought about by a particular use of a substance that was supposed to produce restorative sleep – namely, chloral hydrate. Among the possibilities opened by von Liebig's invention, there was one that did not escape the attention of the petty crims: the fact that its sedative powers grew exponentially when it was mixed with alcohol.[22] This cocktail apparently offered interesting possibilities for those hoping to rob, without too much effort, the night birds who had been foolish enough to let it be known that their pockets were deep.

One of them became so famous for his use of the mixture that it was named after him: Mickey Finn – the manager of the Lone Star Saloon in Chicago, who was accused in 1903 of drugging his wealthy clients so as to relieve them of their money, before dumping them in a nearby alley-way. When they awoke the following morning, plucked and suffering from a terrible headache, the victims of the robbery did not remember a thing; the Mickey Finn offered the double advantage of bringing on sleep and encouraging a very useful amnesia.[23] At least according to urban myth – there is no document establishing formally that Finn engaged in this activity, nor that the name of the drink came from this practice, nor even that this name referred to such a mixture. On the other hand, it has been established that the practice of drugging individuals in bars in order to extract their riches more easily was known, in the United States, from 1869 – just before the discovery of chloral hydrate's sedative properties.[24] Rather than being the reward of the honest man, sleep became a place where new threats lurked – threats that you could do nothing about since, by definition, you were not there to notice them. From supplying being's means of recovery, it became the means of its obliteration – or at least of its enslavement to hostile forces that never stopped trying to assail it, and that only the authorities, on a good day, were able to contain. Whether the urban myth was true or not, refraining from frequenting establishments where events of the type caused by the ingestion of a Mickey Finn might occur was an elementary precaution – despite everything, the night was still seedy.

*

§28. 21st-century working man. Sleep was ambivalent, considered both as something in which good citizens could indulge unreservedly, protected as they were by the vigilance of the forces of order – and as something that still had to pay its dues to the forces of the night. On the one hand, the night had been integrated into the territory under the authority of state forces; on the other, it still had in it a vestige of danger that was enough to warn sensible people from taking the risk – since you never really knew what to expect. The history of the night in the twentieth century was continually pulled between the two terms of this false alternative, as can be seen in the

gradual metamorphosis of nightclubs into places of entertainment cleared of any aspect of political agitation. Even in its most decadent period in the 1970s when cocaine fell from the ceiling of Studio 54 in New York, wrapped in little balloons that had to be burst so that the powder could be sniffed, the excitation was already only on the surface. The nightclub had become a place for containing collective excitement – a means of enabling the 'reproduction of labour power', at a time when it had become possible to rely on certain narcotics to facilitate the task. With cocaine, as with speed or MDMA (two kinds of amphetamines), the question remained one of efficacy – the double efficacy of the orgy itself, and then of what enabled you to recover, so that you could throw yourself into it again next time.[25] The place where this can be seen most clearly is the club that was for a time considered the best in the world: the Berghain in Berlin, opened in 2003 by Michael Teufele and Norbert Thormann in an old electricity plant.[26] In the Berghain, the only things that ever happened were dance and sex – two forms of physical exercise performed in the mechanical aura of techno music, with the help of a fistful of synthetic drugs. If, at least, you were able to convince Sven Marquardt, the most inscrutable bouncer on the planet, that you deserved to enter – which is to say that you deserved to go and work on your relaxation, according to a paradox which nobody seems to have noticed. Where Studio 54 and its emulators (like the Palace, in Paris, at the beginning of the 1980s) were still able to give an illusion of agitation, even if it had become empty, the Berghain no longer makes any pretence: it is nothing but a metaphor for the condition of contemporary labour.

*

§29. The post-nycthemeral hypothesis. Modernity's technical and political colonization of the night is inseparable from the development of industrial capitalism, and from the form of sovereignty associated with it; it ultimately turned it into another form of day. In *24/7*, his furious indictment of capitalism's assault on sleep, Jonathon Crary listed the indications that may lead us to believe that this is just a start – and that some are already imagining pushing the borders of the night even farther back.[27] Among the envisaged scenarios, besides those concerning the possibility

of diverting sunlight to banish darkness once and for all, making 24-hour days possible, we find the notion that we could remove the need for sleep. In the same way that during World War II, the German general staff distributed amphetamine derivatives to Wehrmacht soldiers to get them to advance for several days on end without sleeping, specialists in the American army are becoming interested in certain species of bird that hardly sleep at all. As Crary underscores, these investigations are sure to have reverberations – since we know that what is trialled in the military context tends later to be imported into the civil sphere (as happened with the classifications of the *DSM*).[28] What Crary forgot to mention, however, was that these reverberations can already be heard in the beats to which the dancers move in night-clubs, where the goal of many is to enter into a relationship with time oblivious to the succession of days. Like with the German soldiers in World War II, and those of most other armed forces since, chemical substances contribute to the redistribution of the nycthemeral cycle desired by the party-goers – as though that were its fate. *Get out of the cycle*: this is the shared desire of the dancers, the army officers and the capitalist entrepreneurs; reinvent the cyclical ecology in which the human being has evolved until now, to replace it with another one, shaped to your will. This post-nycthemeral ecology is both the horizon of expectation of a capitalism that seeks to multiply the 'extra time' it extracts from its labour power, and the target of a new market, towards which it has never stopped moving. All time, in the post-nycthemeral age, is destined to become 'extra time' – a time whose only quality is to situate itself beyond that which, in it, does not relate to the obsessional accounting of a pure value, of a value without cost.

*

§30. General somnambulism. 'Insomnia' may have seemed like another word for the attempt to escape the nycthemeral cycle – but it referred to the opposite of what the partisans of industrial, then financial, capitalism desired. Insomnia made you ineffective; it implied the opposite of the efficiency that could be expected of workers – which is why research into how to put an end to it went on all through the twentieth century. The model of the relation to the night that was so popular had nothing to do with the

dazed individual whose excitation needed calming; on the contrary, a kind of tutelage of the excitation in question was what was hoped for. A way of incorporating into labour power the excitation demonstrated by individuals had to be found, in the same way as for their intellectual or physical abilities – for which it constituted, in a certain sense, the intensive measure. Instead of the insomniac, the kind of individual populating the post-nycthemeral ecology should show the same traits as those in another category of subjects – also prisoners of their night, but who were able to ensure that it was without effect: depressives. But the depressive's relation to the night, a pure efficacy without consciousness, an anaesthetic efficacy, had a name – a name that the projects for a total conversion of night into day had given a new currency: *somnambulist*. The somnambulist is anyone who transforms sleep into the site of effective action – whatever means are employed to this end, and whatever the consequences, for the subject and for the recipients. Somnambulism marks the reversal of night into day, its transformation into a site of potential exploitation – even into the model of what every day should be, once it has been given over wholesale to the principle of efficacy. To dispel the last dangers haunting the night, starting with that of collective agitation, it is the night as such that must be eliminated once and for all – or, failing that, the particular type of habitation associated with it, namely sleep. Since it will remain forever impossible to finish *truly* with the night, it is necessary to work towards the transformation of the sleeper into something else, combining the advantages of sleep with those of waking – which is to say, anaesthesia and efficacy. The somnambulist is the ideal candidate – but not the only one.

Chapter 4

Swallowing the Pill

§31. Piracy as method. When, on 10 June 1957, the Food and Drug Administration (FDA) finally authorized the pharmaceutical company G. D. Searle to market Enovid, a new medication for the treatment of menstrual disorders and miscarriages, they did not know what they were about to do.[1] Many years previously, with the guidance (and money) of wealthy veterans of the women's movement, Margaret Sanger, Katharine McKormick and the independent endocrinologist Gregory Pincus had begun the discrete research that would lead to the development of this product. Their research focused on the properties of a particular substance that previous unfinished research had shown to pos-

sess an inhibiting effect on the fertilization of rabbits: progesterone.[2] Pincus had an intuition that if this hormone worked on rabbits, it could have the same effects on humans, which made it possible to imagine a solution to a scourge that post-war America tried very hard to conceal – namely, repeat childbirth. Since in that era even the possibility of controlling births was unimaginable, not to mention methods of contraception other than willpower alone, this research was risky – and, above all, difficult to undertake clinically. Pincus saw to it, therefore, that the trials on the molecule developed with the support of chemists from Searle, who had succeeded in producing a synthetic version of the hormone, were completed a long way from American moral oversight. Thanks to his network in Puerto Rico, he was able to carry out the tests that he had not been able to organize in the United States – even if the results were hardly convincing, and brought to light numerous undesirable effects that forced a large proportion of participants to withdraw.[3] This had no more effect on him than the objections of the Church and the puritans, or the laws of his country; it was enough that a specific point had been established: progesterone did indeed have an inhibiting effect on conception in humans. When Searle received authorization to market Enovid, the FDA were considering, therefore, a medication that had been very little tested and that was still uncertain – and one which was presented as anything but a method of chemical contraception.[4] With a little intelligent communication, however, the news spread like wildfire, finally enabling the tests which had been forbidden until then: the Pill was born.

*

§32. Another scandal. In the years following the release of Enovid, and then its countless competitors, reactions poured in from all directions – some to defend its liberating dimension, others, on the contrary, to express doubts. In 1969, a book by the feminist journalist Barbara Seaman, *The Doctor's Case Against the Pill*, warned consumers of the Pill against the dangers of using it – especially in a disordered way.[5] The scandal provoked by this book, and by that of another journalist, Morton Mintz, titled *The Pill: The Alarming Report*, encouraged the Democrat Senator Gaylord Nelson to organize a series of hearings on the subject in the United States

Senate.[6] These led to a number of recommenda-
tions, amongst which the requirement that the
product be accompanied by precise user directions, indicating how it should be taken, as well
as the risks involved.[7] These hearings did not help
to appease those for whom the Pill represented
an iniquitous intervention into the management
of procreation, still angry at the winning play
Pincus and Searle had made behind their backs.
Their arguments were not without force: not
only did the Pill constitute an intervention that
radically modified the functioning of the body,
but also it inaugurated a new relationship with
medication, since, for the first time in history, it
was taken by individuals who were not ill.[8] In a
certain sense, the opposite was the case: taking
the Pill, a woman in perfect health *made herself ill*
so that the normal, even essential, functioning of
her reproductive organs could be short-circuited
in favour of something else. As a great many fem-
inists have since reminded us, the matter went
beyond the simple limits of the consumers of
Enovid (or any other product); it signalled the
intrusion of a new social concern into the interior
of women's bodies. Suddenly the task of reproduction was replaced by the task of controlling

reproduction – a control that may have been most significant for bringing together individuals pursuing objectives that required women to control themselves. Indeed, it was no surprise that among supporters of the Pill there were many proponents of social eugenics, people like Sanger herself – whose positions on the subject were very close to those of Kraepelin.[9]

*

§33. A little etymology. You have to admit it: the way the Pill worked had a touch of *hacking* about it; after all, it was the first time that the long-term transformation of the hormonal equilibrium of human beings had been attempted on a massive scale. Before the discovery of secretin by William Bayliss and Ernest Starling, in England in 1902, we weren't completely ignorant of the role played by hormones in the functioning of the human body – but the word did not exist: it was invented by Starling in 1905.[10] In Gottingen, in 1849, Arnold Berthold had formulated the hypothesis that there had to be a substance, doubtless carried by the blood, connecting the functioning of the testicles with the expression of masculine characteristics in the rooster. That there should be varieties of

chemical messengers, responsible for transmitting information from one organ to another, as secretin did from the intestine to the pancreas, was not, therefore, a recent discovery – but Starling's term described it best. In the conferences at the Royal College of Physicians in London, during which he introduced the word, he explained the extent to which it, in his view, implied two joint dimensions: a dimension of activity, and a dimension of coordination. A hormone, as the Greek etymology of the word suggests, is a substance that aims to 'activate or excite' an organ, so as to allow coordination between its activity or growth and that of another, situated somewhere else in the body.[11] In the case of progesterone, whose hormonal action was described in 1923, this involves the activation by the ovaries of the rest of the reproductive system so that a normal pregnancy can take place – as well as the excitation of sexual drives. Manipulating progesterone, as was the case with Pincus' formula, means, therefore, manipulating the mode of coordination of the user's organs, in order to reprogramme them for other purposes – or, rather, for no purpose whatsoever. The Pill was a device for disorganizing women's reproductive system – a way of making it dysfunction where it tended to over-perform, of *deactivating* it where it was active, without really taking into account the price to be paid for this deactivation. Because, with the deactivation and discoordination of the ovaries and the uterus, the Pill also moved towards a general deexcitation – a deexcitation that manifested itself immediately, in a great many users, in the collapse of any sexual desire.[12]

*

§34. Excursus on imipramine. All this may recall the way in which antidepressants work – not their mode of therapeutic action, but the way in which they too led to a form of reprogramming based on the anaesthesia of any excitation. This was not by chance: after the era of chloral, the opening of the era of chlorpromazine represented a continuation of the exploration of the world of chemical mediators – since its efficacy was based on the disruption of histamine receptors in the brain. The same went for chlorpromazine's main competitor, imipramine, whose antidepressant properties were discovered in 1957 by the Swiss psychiatrist Ronald Kuhn, after Geigy had begun research on antihistamines which unearthed the

substance from the company's archives.[13] This was not the only company to think that it may be interesting to look at the hidden properties of antihistamines; Merck, for its part, also financed research in this direction – especially after Rhône-Poulenc had discovered the golden goose with chlorpromazine. In any case, as Kuhn explained in a 1959 paper presented at Galesburg State Research Hospital, somewhere in the middle of Illinois, the chemistry of histamines ultimately led to the possibility that the mentally ill could finally 'be well'.[14] By that, he meant that they were unburdened of everything that afflicted them and, therefore, made them unfit for action – and which, above all, prevented them from becoming conscious of their state, in his view the most serious of their symptoms. Not only did imipramine return their smile to individuals who had lost it, but this smile was accompanied by the sudden realization that it had been lost for a long time – even if you had to be clear about the smile in question. This smile did not mean, Kuhn explained, that imipramine should in any way be thought of as a stimulant – it was a substance that was content to eliminate a certain number of symptoms; if there was an activating effect, this was to be linked to this elimination. Things did not change very much with the invention of new generations of antidepressants in the years following the release of chlorpromazine and imipramine; the anticipated effects were the same – and their way of functioning identical. It was always a matter of trying to reorganize the inflow of information in the interior of the brain, so that certain messages that were no longer getting through were now transmitted.[15]

*

§35. Damn you Danes. At the end of September 2016, a group of Danish doctors published, in the online journal *JAMA Psychiatry*, the results of a thirteen-year study into the effects of taking the Pill, which they had carried out on more than a million women between the ages of 24 and 64.[16] The study was motivated by the possibility of discovering a potential link between the use of a hormonal contraception and the fact that depression, in Denmark as in other countries, seemed to affect more women than men. According to the results of their study, it seems that we should now consider it proven that using the Pill does indeed considerably raise (by up to 80 per cent in

the youngest age groups) the risk of depression.[17] As could have been expected, when it appeared the study was received very critically by many representatives of the medical field, who underscored the fact that women were, in any case, more susceptible to depression than men because of the cyclical nature of their hormonal peaks. For them, there was nothing new: the correlation could also have been established with women using other contraception techniques – even with those who do not use anything, since it was above all a biological matter.[18] This was to dismiss a little too quickly the efforts of the Danish team, and to not consider properly the scale of the phenomenon they observed – a phenomenon that had been indicated, moreover, but without being further developed, in the hearings set up by Senator Gaylor in 1970.[19] That the simple possibility of a link between using the Pill and the likelihood of depression should have provoked such hysterical reactions from the medical establishment said a lot about how far beyond the strict framework of individual medication the matter extended. In truth, it was rooted in social and economic politics: what would happen if women ever started to reject the means that had been put at their disposal by those who wanted the best for them – on condition they had the money to pay for it? Because, for those who took a close interest in the functioning of the Pill, depression played an integral part: in the policing of the production of progesterone, it was precisely a question of its *depression* – of making sure that it did not do what would otherwise have been expected of it. As with antidepressants, the Pill worked in the same way as the thing it was fighting against.

*

§36. The hormonal condition. The only difference between the Pill and antidepressants was that the Pill served to reprogramme the hormonal functioning of individuals in perfect health – to alter intentionally a system that was irreproachable except in its performance. Otherwise, it was, in both cases, a question of putting individuals back on the life market who had previously been excluded from it – either because of a 'mental illness', or because of repeat pregnancy – and ensuring that they were able to conduct themselves without causing problems. In truth, however, it looked more like a cleansing operation: its real objective being to transform subjects

into pure acting bodies, reducing anxieties, desires and the risks associated with normal functioning.[20] From this perspective, the Pill's effect could be considered a model: if the anthropology underpinning the present is one of depression, the condition to which this anthropology is subjected is indeed that of hormonal activation. This activation represents the leading edge of narco-capitalist psychopolitical exploration – of the way in which the administration of bodies has been transformed, thanks to the tools made available by modern chemistry, into the administration of the psyche. Psychopolitical reprogramming has become the privileged means for the reintegration of individuals who create disorder in the inner spaces of the world of production – conceived as the default horizon of existence. That it should be without happiness and without desire is the price to be paid if existence is to be spoken of at all; in the age of anaesthesia, there is no existence except as psychic asceticism, bringing together the fate of the body with that of the functions it can fulfil. *Functionalizing the body*: this might be the maxim that best defines the programme of narcocapitalist psychopolitics – so long as it is immediately added that it is a question of a functionalization operating individual by individual, subject by subject. Because, as with the history of the administration of the night and of the chemistry associated with it, as well as with that of the invention of the Pill, the privileged mode of action is based on a form of discoordination, where what counts is what can be counted one by one. The age of anaesthesia is the age of the chemical organization of separation – the age in which every problem must be considered as rooted in the sufferer, without it ever, *ever*, being possible for them to rejoin what lies beyond.

*

§37. The apolitics of contraception. Functionalizing by dysfunction: this was the strange paradox at the heart of the mode of action of the Pill marketed by Searle, and then by all those who subsequently tried to grab parts of his market – the paradox of narcocapitalist psychopolitics. This paradox, however, was only tenable so long as it remained unnoticed, and the possibility never arose that it might constitute a politics, of any kind – at least, a politics doubling that explicitly formulated by its defenders. Whether it was Sanger's eugenic ideas or the standards of

efficacy referred to by the doctors working for the large pharmaceutical groups, there was always, beyond the question of women's liberty, an agenda at work. It was just that this agenda was always dressed up as societal reflection – as a kind of rationalizing discourse for what would otherwise have remained in the domain of what could not be formulated, of what could not, therefore, be managed, of what was dangerous. As when Pincus and Searle presented the authorities with their fait accompli, the doctors who went through the painful experience of the 2016 Danish study thought that the way the Pill worked was self-evident. It went without saying that dealing with contraception hormonally was the best means that those for whom it was important for women to have access to a reliable birth-control technique could have hoped for – nothing was more *objective*. That this should lead to a massive dispossession of the women who used the Pill meant nothing – it was even denied: after all, wasn't the opposite the case, which is to say, the possibility that women could take back possession of their bodies? If you look closely, however, this is indeed what was happening: it was a question of *outsourcing* the definition of the programme governing women's hormonal equilibrium, in the same way that, with 'manic-depressive psychosis', it was a question of *outsourcing* being itself. Tucked away in the grand declarations of social intent, and humanist validations, was a general process of disappropriation that took the form of a reduction of everything to its tautology: a function is a function, a body is a body, and a being is a being. Narcocapitalist psychopolitics presented itself as an apolitical functionalization, while taking politics into the heart of ontology.

*

§38. *Elements of anti-ontology.* When she published *Testo Junkie* in 2008, Beatriz Preciado (who has since become Paul Preciado) showed that for some the paradox had not gone unnoticed – and that it was high time that the tautology on which the hormonal condition was based was confronted.[21] In order to avoid the traps deployed by the pharmaceutical industry, and the actors of narcocapitalist psychopolitics more generally, the time had come to start to dissociate what they had claimed to associate. Once it was understood that hormones constituted the logistical network through which the body goes about the coordination of its organs, and the activation of their functions, it was absurd to continue to allow someone else to mess around with them, playing the role of programmer unbeknown to those affected. From a means of expropriation of the self in the form of a reduction of the body to efficient being, hormones could become the tool for the exploration of a metamorphosis that orients the body towards horizons that were not those of efficacy, activity or 'being well'. Not only could they serve to redefine the relationship to gender identity, as Preciado herself experienced (an experience written up in *Testo Junkie*), but they authorized all possible reconnections between organs and functions. Hormones could enable the disruption of everything on which narcocapitalist psychopolitics rests – in that it bases itself on the attempt to monopolize the factors defining the hormonal condition, even if no hormone is involved.[22] To do this, you would have to invent completely new uses (which means taking on new knowledge), while exploring ways of getting around large pharmaceutical groups or government agencies in order to produce them. Getting away from the 'pharmacopornography' that Preciado speaks of could only be done through

the invention of hormonal *hacking* techniques to
compete with those already implemented by the
inventors of the Pill, establishing a new front line
where consensus had seemed to prevail.[23] The
ontological objectivity of the upholders of the
hormonal condition would then give way to a
form of anti-ontology – a strategy of collapsing
the foundations of psychopolitical discourse, in
which every function becomes dysfunction, and
every being, its own ruin. The being you had to be
has never really been; it was nothing other than a
category of order to which to subject individuals.

*

§39. *Hormones and hacktivism.* Preciado's message
was heard; in 2015, the manifesto 'xénoféministe',
published on their internet site by the collective
Laboria Cuboniks, even made it an article of
faith: hormonal *hacking* was to become an instrument of the resistance.[24] This, however, was to
be accompanied by a supplementary manoeuvre:
the establishment at home of the means of producing the hormones in question – to bring an
end to the monopoly (and forms) instituted by
industrial capitalism. The militants of Laboria
Cuboniks were not alone in advocating the

expansion of DIY in the sphere of hormones; artists Mary Maggic and Byron Rich may, among others, be counted amongst those experimenting in this area.[25] If Maggic, something of a scrapper, was able to make her own contraceptive pills to mitigate the difficulties of getting hold of them during her travels, this was because anyone could do it so long as he (or she, as it happens) had the information to hand. These are just two examples demonstrating not only how Preciado's contentions were taken seriously by actors in an emerging alternative hormonal scene, but that this scene had chosen activism as its paradigm for action. Once again, this shows how far the issue extends beyond the framework of medicine, to encompass a whole set of political and economic concerns, implicating all the subjects of narcocapitalist psychopolitics – along with their environment. Indeed, the consumption of hormones constitutes the first step in an ecological circuit redistributing what has been consumed according to the way in which it is evacuated: hormones are pissed out, and circulate with piss, to become a new form of pollution.[26] Far from being of concern only to the people taking it, the Pill is a symptom of a general state of the world, where the anthropology, economy and ecology characterizing the age of anaesthesia, as the age of the dazed disorganization of subjects, come together. Making the Pill into an opportunity for an anti-ontological experience or reprogramming being into something that refuses being, as suggested by Preciado, was a way of *screwing* the smooth running of the anaesthetic programme. But this screwing had a downside, which the propositions of Laboria Cuboniks or the DIY artists revealed: it continued to count only individual by individual.

*

§40. Bigger than us. The Pill discoordinates and disactivates – but that is not all it does: it deexcites as well; it undertakes the recentring of subjects on the being that they are supposed to be, and on the task that, as being, they are supposed to carry out – which is to say, on their work or their social or familial role. The erring that so frightened Kraepelin was also what worried certain champions of the Pill, horrified by the spectacle of so many women unable to control their sexuality (or that of their partner), and so ruining themselves prematurely. The Pill's interest, in

their view, was therefore that it enabled them to find a solution to a massive waste of resources, a human expenditure without return, a pure excess that they could not help thinking could be put to good use. Excitation, or the phenomenon of an intense exit from the self, was what had to be disposed of: it was a question of putting this waste in order, transforming it into investment. Every action had to count – instead of getting lost in useless gesticulations that would require the intervention of forces that could have been better used elsewhere, as was the case for the sick calmed thanks to injections of chloral hydrate. Chemical anaesthesia was the best way of doing this: by detaching subjects from what allowed them to perceive, and so feel, the play of forces that pushed them outside themselves, it brought them back to a level from which to achieve the greatest efficacy. It was an efficacy that was disturbed by nothing, except, perhaps, various biological necessities it was difficult to pretend did not exist – like the nycthemeral rhythm, which it was nonetheless believed could be drawn out. This may seem like a nightmare from the imagination of a writer partial to dystopias – but only really when it is presented in this light; the rest of the time, it has very aptly been called 'everyday life'. The 'everyday life' that the subjects of the age of anaesthesia experience, however, is more like a succession of grey moments with high levels of nervousness, within which accidents sometimes occur suggesting that things could be different. But there are only two ways in which this can happen: either through the quest of a subject nurturing the suspicion that anaesthesia is not destiny, or through contamination by an excitation that is bigger than us.

Chapter 5

The Politics of Overexcitement

§41. A forgotten bestseller. During 1891, the table of contents of *Archivio di psichiatria sociale*, the journal edited by the criminologist Cesare Lombroso, carried on two occasions the name Scipio Sighele – a 23-year-old researcher who taught criminal law at the University of Pisa.[1] The two articles bearing his name quickly made Sighele the subject of conversation. He was, at least, sufficiently spoken about for an editor to publish a book-length version of them, released that same year, under the title *La folla delinquente*; it was a global bestseller.[2] In the guise of a study in 'social psychology', Sighele's book gave expression to a concern shared by cultured individuals the world over: one brought on by the appearance

of a new entity in the social cartography. This entity, which everyone agreed was characterized by its irritability and its irrationality, was none other than the modern crowd, that aggregate of individuals born of the urbanization associated with the development of industrial capitalism in western countries. For refined souls, the nebulous magma of frustrated instincts making up the substance of the popular masses could only constitute a danger: as confirmed by the recent revolutions, you never really knew what to expect from it. Sighele's success came from his being the first to try to give a more or less legitimate face to this concern, and to provide the scientific lexicon that could euphemize what was above all a class reflex to the discovery of a new threat. *With crowds, anything is possible*: this was the main lesson that the young criminologist took from his observations, and from discussion of the principal reflections available on the subject at the time – those of Herbert Spencer, for example, or Gabriel Tarde.[3] From Spencer (the first of these two), he took up and slightly modified the idea that it was possible to consider that the collective being presented, from the psychological perspective, more than a simple analogy with the individual being; the crowd is not a simple aggregate, it is a thing as such.[4] From the second, he retained that the main characteristic of this thing in itself was its dangerousness: if crowds are irrational and irritable, what they are capable of, which could be anything, necessarily tends towards the criminal act – and, therefore, because we are dealing with the masses, impunity.[5] This was what required that an attempt be made to understand crowds: to bring to an end the impunity on which they were able to count.

*

§42. From apprehension to implication. That the crowd was delinquent by necessity is a thesis that should not surprise us coming from the pen of someone who presented himself as a disciple of Enrico Ferri, one of the three founders, with Lombroso, of the positivist school of criminology.[6] The members of this school were obsessed by the meticulous listing of everything that could enable the establishment of the determining causes of criminal phenomena – the way in which a set of circumstances or characteristics lead immediately to the crime. Where Lombroso, Ferri and their colleagues were primarily interested

in individuals, it fell to Sighele to inaugurate the field of criminal research into collective matters – research that led to many further vocations. Amongst the first to follow the intuitions of the young researcher, we find the name of Tarde himself, who echoed his work at a conference held in Brussels in 1892, titled 'Le crime des foules' ['The Crime of Crowds'], the tone of which was as apprehensive as that of Sighele's book.[7] The publication of the conference paper the following year in *La Revue des deux mondes* encouraged Sighele to strike up a correspondence with the sociologist, the most important elements of which were published in 1901 in the second edition of the French translation of *The Delinquent Crowd*.[8] The ten-year interval separating the two publications, however, saw Sighele's positions, like those of Tarde, develop in a direction that neither would have foreseen at the time: the anxiety that had guided their initial research evolved as they went along into a positive interest.[9] Maybe it was a result of their dialogue – but the crux of the matter was that this new being that was the crowd could be considered not only as a simple mass of individual drives capable of anything and everything. This capacity, such as it was, already indicated that something else was at stake in mass phenomena, which could only relate to pure force; in a book also published in 1901, titled *L'opinion et la foule* [*Opinion and Crowds*], Tarde called this something else 'interest'.[10] Where the crowds described by Sighele, and then Gustave Le Bon – whose 1895 book *Psychologie des foules* [*Crowd Psychology*] was nothing but a plagiary of the Italian's – were characterized by the forgetting of self to which each individual was victim, the 'public' that interested Tarde offered everyone the opportunity of exploring the passionate interests that had encouraged them to come together.[11]

*

§43. The madness of crowds. Despite this slippage, suggesting room for optimism amid the danger of crowds, there was an element that, from Sighele's first articles to Tarde's book, never changed: the term for the energy characterizing the life of crowds. As Sighele had suggested, if a crowd was only ever a larger-scale body with its own psychic life, this term could apply equally as well to individual psychology as to collective psychology – the term was 'excitation'. As he differentiated

the concept of the 'public' he introduced in *Opinion and Crowds*, Tarde recalled the extent to which crowds never stop oscillating between the 'two extreme poles of excitation and depression' – 'like madmen', he added.[12] He did not clarify what he meant by that, as though the concept of excitation was so self-evident that it was possible to spare the definition; speaking of the excitation of crowds, even just of excitation, was a psycho-logical and physiological commonplace. Indeed, in the description of collective movements, the word 'excitation' already had a history, in which it had shared the stage with another word in the restless passive: the word 'enthusiasm' – that emotion of believers seized by a force that exceeds them.[13] While enthusiasm had been used to describe the particular type of sublime asso-ciated with revolutionary events (this was how Immanuel Kant and Edmund Burke understood it), the use of 'excitation' was a little different. In 1869, Gustave Flaubert could still speak of the enthusiasm that Frédéric Moreau, the hero of *L'éducation sentimentale*, had witnessed in his participation in the events of the 1848 revolution – and which, through contagion, he himself had felt.[14] But, at the end of the nineteenth century, the logic was reversed: enthusiasm was the affect of possession by a foreign force, and excitation was more associated with the stimulation of interior forces – a kind of mobilization of the self, for which the outside was just a pretext. This was what had fascinated the theorists of crowds: the way in which individuals, when they came together, went out of themselves, voluntarily expelling themselves from their own selves to get lost in an aggregate, of which they were no longer even members. Excitement signified a change of state – a passage from a state of rest to a state of activity characterized by an increased level of energy.

*

§44. *Epistemology of passage.* That excitation should turn up in the centre of the theoretical machinery established by the crowd 'psychologist' could be explained by the fact that, as opposed to enthusiasm, it had a lineage that was already scientific. As Sighele recalled in *The Delinquent Crowd*, excitation pointed to something that was above all physical – bodily even, as can be seen in the way Spencer based his own analyses on a transposition of 'Charcot's physiological law'.[15] According to this law, muscular activity, such as that 'excited' by an exterior force, is immediately translated into a modification of the mental states in the actor, in such a way that all physical excitation immediately turns into psychic excitation.[16] It was handy: thanks to the concept of excitation, it became possible to transit without difficulty from the physical to the psychic, then from the collective to the individual, once it had been understood that the heart of the operation is change of state, the passage from one state to another. Excitation is what enabled the crossing of borders (conceptual as well as material) that would not have been crossed without it; it enacted the dis-enclosure of what had been enclosed, the de-limitation of what had been limited. The only element that remained constant in the passage from one domain to another was the increase in the intensive state of what had been traversed – from the muscles to the brain, then from the individual brain to what took place in the case of crowds. For observers of the life of groups, nothing was more worrying than this: if every crossing of a border implied an increase in the energy level of what was excited, you had to conclude that there was a risk of very quickly losing control. From this perspective, Sighele was in agreement with Kraepelin when the latter insisted on the necessity of always keeping patients suffering from 'manic-depressive psychosis' calm, to avoid the whole hospital becoming a battle field. With clinical psychiatry, as with social psychology, the greatest danger was the gradual contamination of neighbouring spaces by an operator supremely capable of crossing into them – and that did so by nature. If political activity had a sense, it consisted above all in suppressing excitation, and making sure that what belonged to two different orders continued to remain separated.

*

§45. *Freud to the rescue.* In the years following the publication of the second edition of *The Delinquent Crowd*, and *Opinion and Crowds*, the paranoid infatuation with the image of the excited crowd did not run dry – helped, it is true, by an increasingly turbulent history. Sigmund Freud played a bit-part when, in 1921, he published a long essay titled *Massenpsychologie und Ich-Analyse*, in which he took up the vulgarization of Sighele's thesis by Gustave Le Bon, to give it new interpretation.[17] Despite his claim to ground it in desire, and its connection with the constitution of human narcissism, he still ended up recycling the clichés burnished by his forebears – while adding a little pop-mythology. What was at stake in crowds, for Freud, was nothing other than the unexpected re-emergence of what he called the 'primal horde' – namely, the primitive state of the human being in groups, haunted by the spectre of the 'primal father' that the said horde considers the 'ego ideal'.[18] That is to say, Freud clarified, a kind of potlatch takes place in the passage from the individual to the crowd – the exchange of the ego ideal elaborated by the individual as a basic ingredient in the constitution of their narcissism, for that embodied in the leader. We have to conclude, therefore, that, from the perspective of the psychic life, the abandoning of the 'primal horde', which makes a return in the crowd, was rooted in a symptomatology that was not far removed from that of manic-depressive psychosis.[19] Why? Quite simply because it is characteristic of melancholia, in its manic phases, to see the subject's ego rebel against the demands of their ego ideal – in such a way that it may want to turn towards another that is more suitable. Of course, as he was coming to this conclusion, Freud could not stop himself from taking up the vocabulary of excitation: if the ego ended up turning against its ego ideal, this was because, he wrote, it was 'excited into rebellion by its mistreatment, coming from its ideal'.[20] Tarde's hypothesis, put forward on one page of *Opinion and Crowds*, suggesting that the life of crowds can be understood as an oscillation between mania and depression, finds, therefore, confirmation in Freud: the man of the crowd is a depressive in manic phase. Only a mention of chloral hydrate (or another sedative product of the same stripe) was missing for the analogy with Kraepelin's analysis of 'manic-depressive psychosis' to be complete.

*

§46. Being no one. Freud, it seems, did not take on board Tarde's distinction between the 'crowd' and the 'public'; he was happy to maintain a negative, drive-based definition of the collective life of individuals – and the conception of excitation it required. He was not the only one: in the years following the publication of *Group Psychology and the Analysis of the Ego*, countless authors followed a similar line in their interpretation – including

Wilhelm Reich, Elias Canetti, Hermann Broch and José Ortega y Gasset.[21] In every case, it was possible to discern a nostalgia for a world where the individual was as rare as it was rational – a world, in short, where the status of individual was reserved for those who did not allow themselves to yield when confronted by their ego ideal, which was inevitably masculine and bourgeois. The individual was a man who did not fear his ego ideal, because he knew that his ego was not so far removed from it, even coinciding almost completely with it; the individual was a man whose narcissism was strong enough to rest on nothing but itself. Such an individual, it went without saying, would never allow himself to indulge in the expression of narcissistic collapse implied by participation in crowd action; he felt neither the need nor the desire – his position placed him above fragile narcissistic excitations. That this figure, in which there was a perfect coincidence between the ego and the ego ideal, represented a perfect nightmare did not seem to bother Freud very much – who, it is true, had organized his whole life according to a highly determined programming of the ego ideal. It was perhaps this desire *to be someone* that led to his dislike of crowds, and to his refusal to see anything in them but the lure of the primal horde, and what, in that, was born of resentment. It was true that, even in the positive interpretation that Tarde came to in the end – that of the 'public' – abandonment of the ambition to be someone constituted the first condition for the formation of a new entity: participation in the crowd always implied a transformation into *no one* [*personne*]. Amongst the countless transformations that excitation might produce, that is, you had to include that by which an individual became a no one [*une personne*] – became anyone, became a dividual. The passage from the individual to the crowd signalled the passage from an ontology to its contrary – to an anti-ontology whose primary characteristic was the abandonment of being.

*

§47. What's good for you. Being is the objective partner of all police; it is the category on which any enterprise aiming at establishing an order in which places can be assigned with certainty is based and it plays the role of anthropological standard and existential horizon.[22] In contemporary narcocapitalism, this is a standard of

depression, understood as the deflation of excitation, and the horizon is that of the chemical reorganization through which this deflation can be converted into a rule of efficacy. *Being is the site of psychopolitics*; there is no being outside the business of ordering the affects separating subjects from everything in them pertaining to the dysfunctional – everything, at least, that is considered as such in the rules and regulations of narcocapitalism. Meaning that, in psychocapitalism, ontology becomes the site of commandment – being becomes the site of what has-to-be, the *esti*, which Giorgio Agamben spoke of, the site of *esto*, while the fact becomes the site of the norm, and so on, in a kind of monstrous precipitation in which the state and order of things are indistinguishable.[23] But this indistinctness, far from presenting itself as the management operation that it really is, puts itself forward as a *solution* – as a way of regulating everything in *your* life that was deregulated, and that made *you* so unhappy, so much in disagreement with *your*-self. Being, in psychopolitics, is the gift offered to all those who feel disjointed, to whom the possibility of a continuity solution is presented as the most desirable thing there is; being would be the re-membering that the dis-membered so longs for. By contrast, excitation would be the process by which this re-membering is prevented; it would be what makes the reconstitution of the being of subjects impossible – or rather, what makes the reorganization according to being's designs impossible. The warning had been clear: *ex-citare*, as Kraepelin knew, signified 'carrying outside the self', expelling from being's limits, within which it was understood that it would be better to confine yourself, if you wanted to avoid the decomposition brought on by depression. *The only being is disexcited* – as, moreover, a long tradition had not stopped hammering home to dissipated spirits, which is to say, to anyone who did not want to be the loyal customer of those who know *what's good for you*. Where excitation reigns, they have always insisted, being cannot take place; where excitation reigns, there is only *désêtre*.

*

§48. *The juridicity of excitation.* Maybe we should go further – excitation is not only exit from self, setting in motion, displacement of what is fixed, change of state; it is also the operation by which this displacement is performed: the invocation or the provocation. In Roman juridical vocabulary, excitation could also refer to the action by which it was possible to come to the division of goods making up an estate, or to that by which an individual could be called to justice.[24] In the tenth volume of *Histoire romaine*, Titus Livius has consul Publius Decius Mus using the term in around 340 BCE during a speech he gave to the Senate on his election – the capacity to excite was what designated the free man.[25] *To be excited, is to be called to the tribunal* – it is to see one's being and actions subjected to a court of justice; it is to put one's being to the test of an outside whose decisions were liable to redound on you, for the better or for the worse. The fact that excitation constitutes being's tribunal explains why the theorists of crowds, the doctors of depression, the police of the night, and birth-control activists alike have always distrusted it. Far from being only a disruption from which being is at liberty to protect itself, excitation embodies a form of accusation – a way of addressing being so as to hold it accountable for what it is, for what it rests on and for where it is heading. You could even say that excitation is being's disquiet, that which prevents it from being able to settle down in the satisfied comfort of its self-identification – it represents the return of anxiety where calm should reign. But that there should be a connection between this anxiety and the state of liberty, even if it is understood in the very restrained terms of the Roman Republic, adds a crucial nuance to what constitutes the essence of excitation: to be unsatisfied is *also* to be free. On the other hand, to shut yourself away in the satisfaction of being is to abjure one of the prerogatives of the free man, and to resolve yourself to someone else, somewhere else, deciding for you – making liberty into a signifier without content, a kind of rhetorical talisman. It is, moreover, in this way that excitation is understood by all those for whom it must be pitilessly combatted: with the trial of the exit from self, the whole order based on the promotion of the self's being is put into question – is called to justice.

*

§49. On the contrary. When he opposed the 'public' to the 'crowd', and therefore the logic of the deepening of impassioned interests to that of their dissolution in a continuum of anonymous

tension, Tarde further underscored the modern mistrust of excitation. It was all the more curious since he had himself insisted several times on the fact that there was a regime of intensity of excitation in which it turned into its opposite – becoming, that is, the catalyst of impassioned interests giving rise to the public. He called this regime of intensity 'overexcitation'; there is overexcitation when the movement of excitation becomes such that a kind of liberation phenomenon is produced – in the same way that we speak of the possibility of 'liberation' from terrestrial attraction.[26] In truth, Tarde was more measured: the three occurrences of the word 'overexcitation' in *Opinion and Crowds* could even be read as so many paroxysmal expressions of the fear likely to be provoked by excitation in general. But Tarde's discomfort was already a sign that something else was at stake in the lexicological hesitations he displayed – something other than distrust, which, perhaps, belonged more to the sphere of fascination. Overexcitement, as the culmination of a process of exiting the self, could be seen as a modern version of the amok – the murderous fury that in certain Malaysian tribes can overtake an individual – just as much as of its opposite. The temptation to stick with the first interpretation was strong: Kraepelin himself published in 1904 the account of a journey to Bali in which he compared the amok to the mania he had observed in patients afflicted with 'manic-depressive psychosis'.[27] It was, however, possible to consider that Tarde's interest in anything that seemed to be a process of enlargement of the circles of involvement within which individuals fell must necessarily lead to a re-evaluation of excitation. For him 'overexcitation' perhaps indicated the place where you could envisage encountering the energy on which rested the possibility of the enlargement in question – the fact that impassioned interests led to ever-larger aggregations. For Tarde, 'overexcitation' indicated the power of contamination proper to the abandonment of any identification with being – its potential virality.

*

§50. Amok politics. Every crowd tends to get bigger; every crowd tends to go beyond its own limits to include an ever-greater number of individuals, inevitably; excitation is the name given to the principle of contamination that enables

this inclusion. While, for Tarde, this could only concern the 'public', the variety of crowd that he freed from being a crowd, it was in fact what characterized every form – as all those for whom they represented a kind of foil understood so well. *The only politics is the politics of excitation* – and every attempt to finish with it must be understood as an attempt to finish with politics – to ensure that politics, as a means of putting the being of individuals to the test, should not take place.[28] Indeed, as narcocapitalism developed, it never stopped arguing for the need to make all politics impossible, through the promotion of an anthropology from which all excitation could be stripped – and with it, the possibility of its viralization. The promotion of being at the heart of this anthropology was nothing but the first phase of a gesture of annihilation of anything that might resemble an experience of the outside or an exit movement. The upholders of this anthropology knew it: the withdrawal inside the limits of being signified the end of any possible political agitation – once it is understood that politics, as excitation, necessarily implies deidentification, the surpassing of being. Politics is anything that leads to the collapse of being, everything that shows instability, lability, permeability, incon-sistency; politics is anything that continues to escape the regime of order through which being can be instituted or guaranteed. Saying that there is no politics except of excitation is therefore the same as saying that there is no politics except of *désêtre* – there is only politics of the amok, of what escapes the control through which subjects find themselves constrained in the limits of being. The idea that politics would be a rational affair, with which subjects freed from the movements of excitation would be compatible, is the favourite mantra of narcocapitalism – what best assures its hold on the subjects in question, what establishes them as subjects. If we want to get shot of it, we should, therefore, first get shot of this idea, then of all of its accompanying psychopolitical acces-sories, to finally come to terms with what forms the mad foundation of every human grouping – a madness which is the only thing that can give us hope.

Epilogue

Gettin' Up

§51. The age of anexcitation. On the day that Morton and Jackson filed their patent request for the new surgical assistance technique they had discovered, they did something of which the importance cannot be overestimated: they laid the foundations for a new conception of the subject. For centuries, pain had been an obstacle that no surgeon could get around – a kind of wall like the one plane builders had been coming up against for so long.[1] This wall could be thought of in several ways, but to surgeons only one was really important: the pain felt by patients during the operation they were undergoing made them uncontrollable. More than the incompetence of the surgeon, it was the cries and movements of

the person lying on the operating table, who was experiencing this period as the torture that it was, which could result in catastrophe.[2] Thanks to the method discovered by Morton and Jackson, this concern could be swept aside; now, calm reigned in the operating room, allowing the surgeon to practise his art without the patient's soul- (or body-) searching interfering with his work. Anaesthesia had transformed individuals into subjects, through the intervention of a chemical technique that led to the bracketing of everything that, in them, belonged to the world of 'excitation' – the word was often used by pioneers of the method.[3] Rather than as the opening of the age of anaesthesia, perhaps it would be better to speak of the opening of the age of anexcitation – the age of the ablation of individuals' animation principle, transforming them into simple bodies, subject to examination and manipulation. *Thanks to anaesthesia, surgeons had peace*: an anaesthetized body is a body that causes no bother – a body that at last coincides with itself, which is to say with what is expected of it in the context of its operability, its capacity for being operated on. To become the subject of an operation is to become, therefore, more or less organized matter, a material mass of organs and flesh available for fixing, repair, amputation, observation and so on.[4] Now, at the same time, a new word appeared in political vocabulary, a word used to designate what we ended up calling 'crowds': the word 'masses'. This was not by chance; behind the transformation of the subject into matter, something else was happening. Crowds had to become matter so that you could forget that they had a soul.

Notes

Prologue

1 See Roger Dachez, *Histoire de la médecine, de l'Antiquité à nos jours* [*History of Medicine: From Antiquity to the Present*], 2nd edn (Paris: Taillandier, 2012) p. 587. For more detail, see Marguerite Zimmer, *Histoire de l'anesthésie: Méthodes et techniques au XIXe siècle* [*History of Anesthesia: Methods and Techniques in the 19th Century*] (Les Ulis: EDP Sciences, 2008) p. 64.

2 Dachez, *Histoire de la médecine*, p. 586.

3 *Ibid.*, p. 588.

4 See Miriam Rossiter Small, *Oliver Wendell Holmes* (New York: Twayne, 1962) p. 55. Cited by https://en.wikipedia.org/wiki/History_of_general_anesthesia.

1 Welcome to Prozacland

1 See Jacques Postel and Claude Quétel, *Nouvelle histoire de la psychiatrie* [*A New History of Psychiatry*] (Paris: Dunod, 2012) p. 224.

2 'Habilitation' refers to the qualification to conduct autonomous university teaching and is crucial to obtaining a professorship in universities in many European countries, particularly Germany, Austria and Switzerland [trans. note].

3 *Ibid.*, p. 225.

4 *Ibid.*, p. 343.

5 *Ibid.*, p. 225. See also Jacques Hochmann, *Histoire de la psychiatrie* (Paris: Presses universitaires de France, 2015) p. xx.

6 Emil Kraepelin, *Manic-Depressive Insanity and Paranoia* [1913], trans. R. Mary Barclay (Edinburgh: E. & S. Livingstone, 1921).

7 *Ibid.*

8 See Claude Quétel, *Histoire de la folie, de l'Antiquité à nos jours* [*History of Madness: From Antiquity to the Present*], 2nd edn (Paris: Taillander, 2012). See also Claude Minois, *Histoire du mal de vivre: De la mélancolie à la dépression* [*History of Unhappyness: From Melancholia to Depression*] (Paris: La Martinière, 2003); *Mélancolies: De l'Antiquité au XXe siècle* [*Melancholies: From Antiquity to the 20th Century*], ed. Yves Hersant (Paris: Robert Laffont, 2005); Patrick Dandrey, *Anthologie de l'humeur noire: Écrits sur la mélancolie, d'Hippocrate à l'Encyclopédie* [*Anthology of Black Humour: Writings on Melancholia, from*

Hippocrates to the Encyclopedia] (Paris: Gallimard, 2005).

9 See Martin Brüne, 'On Self-Domestication, Psychiatry, and Eugenics', *Philosophy, Ethics, and Humanities*, 2, 21, 2007, online.

10 Kraepelin, *Manic-Depressive Insanity.*

11 *Ibid.*

12 See David Healy, *The Antidepressant Era* (Cambridge, MA: Harvard University Press, 1999).

13 *Ibid.*

14 On all this, see William H. Brock, *Justus von Liebig: The Chemical Gatekeeper* (Cambridge: Cambridge University Press, 1997).

15 See Jean-Noël Missa, *Naissance de la psychiatrie biologique: Histoire des traitements des maladies mentales au XXe siècle* [*The Birth of Biological Psychiatry: History of the Treatment of Mental Illnesses in the 20th Century*] (Paris: Presses universitaires de France, 2006) p. 65.

16 See 'exciter', in *Le Robert, Dictionnaire historique de la langue française*, ed. Alain Rey, vol.I: *A/E* (Paris: Le Robert, 2016) p. 1356.

17 See Healy, *The Antidepressant Era.*

18 *Ibid.*

19 *Ibid.*

20 *Ibid.*

21 *Ibid.*

22 *Ibid.*

23 *Ibid.*

24 See Mark Fisher, *Ghosts of My Life: Writings on Depression, Hauntology and Lost Futures* (Alresford: Zero, 2014).

25 *Ibid.*, p. 375.

26 For a complete list, see https://en.wikipedia.org/wiki/
Antidepressant#Adverse_effects.

27 The updated list can be downloaded from the
WHO site: www.who.int/medecines/publications/
essentialmedicines/18th_EML.pdf.

28 https://en.wikipedia.org/wiki/Diagnostic_and_Statisti
cal_Manual_of_Mental_Disorders.

29 See Healy, *The Antidepressant Era*.

30 The concept of psychopolitics was shaped in 1955 by
Kenneth Goff, a militant anti-communist Christian,
who credited its invention to Lavrenti Beria, the infa-
mous head of the NKVD – who apparently gave the
following definition in a manual to be used by ancillar-
ies: 'The art and science of asserting and maintaining
domination over the thoughts and feelings of loyalty
of individuals, leaders, offices and the masses, and
the achievement of the conquest of enemy nations
through "mental curing".' Peter Sloterdijk made
it one of the central concepts in his work, without
ever specifying the meaning; more recently, Byung
Chul-han suggested a use directed explicitly against
Michel Foucault's concept of 'biopolitics': Byung
Chul-han, *Psychopolitik: Neoliberalismus und die neuen
Machttechniken* (Frankfurt: S. Fischer Verlag, 2014).

2 Narcocapitalism Unlimited

1 See Zimmer, *Histoire de l'anesthésie*, p. 70.

2 On the history of the discovery of cocaine, see Paul
Gootenberg, *Andean Cocaine: The Making of a Global*

Drug (North Carolina: University of North Carolina Press, 2009).

3 *Ibid.*

4 *Ibid.*

5 See Jean-Pierre Bailliart and Michel Faure, 'Sigmund Freud et la naisance de l'anesthésie locale en ophtalmologie', *Histoire des sciences médicales*, 19, 1, 1985, p. 30.

6 Sigmund Freud, 'À propos de la coca' ['On Cocaine'], in *Un peu de cocaïne pour me délier la langue* [*A Little Cocaine to Untie my Tongue*], trans. into French by Marielle Roffi (Paris: Max Milo, 2005) p. 35. On what follows, see Florence Coblence, 'Freud et la cocaïne', *Revue française de psychanalyse*, 66, 2, 2002, p. 371.

7 Freud, 'À propos de la coca'.

8 *Ibid.*, p. 48.

9 *Ibid.*, p. 54.

10 *Ibid.*, p. 57.

11 *Ibid.*, p. 50.

12 *Ibid.*, p. 48, n. 44.

13 See Gootenberg, *Andean Cocaine*.

14 See H. Richard Friman, 'Germany and the Transformations of Cocaine, 1860–1920', in *Cocaine: Global Histories*, ed. Paul Gootenberg (London and New York: Routledge, 1999) p. 83.

15 Freud, 'À propos de la coca', p. 69.

16 See Gootenberg, *Andean Cocaine*.

17 *Ibid.*

18 See Norman Ohler, *Blitzed: Drugs in Nazi Germany*, trans. Shaun Whiteside (London: Penguin, 2016).

19 *Ibid.*

20 *Ibid.*

21 Aymon de Lestrange, *Angelo Mariani, 1838–1914: Le vin de coca et la naissance de la publicité moderne* [*Angelo Mariani, 1838-1914: Coca Wine and the Birth of Modern Advertising*] (Paris: Intervals, 2016) p. 29.

22 *Ibid.*, p. 30.

23 *Ibid.*, p. 70.

24 *Ibid.*, p. 138.

25 See Mark Pendergast, *For God, Country & Coca-Cola: The Definitive History of the Great American Soft Drink and the Company that Makes it*, 3rd edn (New York: Basic Books, 2013) p. 20. For a more polemical account, see William Reymond, *Coca-Cola: L'enquête interdite* [*Coca-Cola: The Forbidden Enquiry*] (Paris: Flammarion, 2006) p. 44, which adds a few new elements to Pendergast's account.

26 Pendergast, *For God, Country & Coca-Cola*, p. 53.

27 *Ibid.*, p. 43.

28 On Anslinger, read John C. McWilliams, *The Protectors: Anslinger and the Federal Bureau of Narcotics (1930–1962)* (Newark: University of Delaware Press, 1990).

29 *Ibid.*, p. xx.

30 This, at least, was the thesis put forward by Antonio Maria Costa, the Director of the United Nations Office on Drugs and Crime, in an interview in the *Observer* on 13 December 2009. See Rajeev Sival, 'Drug Money Saved Banks in Global Crisis, Claims UN Advisor', *Guardian*, 13 December 2009. To date, the proof that Costa claimed to have has not been made public. See Joras Ferwarda, 'The Effects of Money Laundering', in

Research Handbook on Money Laundering, ed. Brigitte Unger and Daan van der Linde (Cheltenham and Northampton: Edward Elgar, 2013) p. 40.

31 See Friman, 'Germany and the Transformations of Cocaine', p. 90.

32 Sigmund Freud, 'Lettres de Freud à Martha' ['Letters from Freud to Martha'], in *Un peu de cocaïne*, p. 17.

33 See Johann Hari, *Chasing the Scream: The First and Last Days of the War on Drugs* (London: Bloomsbury, 2016). On the consequences of the 'war on drugs' in the Andes, see Frédéric Faux, *Coca! Une enquête dans les Andes* (Arles: Actes Sud, 2015).

34 On the history and the significance of the end of the Bretton-Woods system, see Yanis Varoufakis, *And the Weak Suffer What They Must? Europe, Austerity, and the Threat to Global Stability* (London: Bodley Head, 2016); Peter Sloterdijk, *Après nous le déluge: Les temps modernes comme expérience antigénéalogique* [*After Us, The Deluge: Modern Times as an Antigenealogical Experience*], trans. into French by Olivier Mannoni (Paris: Payot, 2016) p. 178.

35 Roberto Saviano, *Extra pure: Voyage dans l'économie de la cocaïne,* trans. into French by Vincent Raynaud (Paris: Gallimard, 2014). (NB. The English edition was published with the title *Zerozerozero: Look at Cocaine and All You See Is Powder. Look Through Cocaine and You See the World* (New York: Penguin, 2015).)

3 Day Without End

1 Oscar Liebreich, *Das Chloralhydrat: Ein neues Hypnoticum und Anaestheticum und dessen Anwendung in der Medicin; eine Arzneimittel-Untersuchung* (Berlin: Müller, 1869).

2 See Guillaume Garnier, *L'oubli des peines: Une histoire du sommeil (1700–1850)* [*Forgetting Anguish: A History of Sleep (1700–1850)*] (Rennes: Presses universitaires de Rennes, 2013) p. 188.

3 *Ibid.*, p. 195. See also Christian Le Marec, 'Histoire de l'opium médicinale: Du pavot aux alcaloïdes de opium' ['History of Medicinal Opium: From the Poppy to Opium Alkaloids'], *Douleurs: évaluation – diagnostique – traitements*, 5, 2, 2004, p. 83.

4 Garnier, *L'oubli des peines*, p. 182.

5 *Ibid.*, pp. 187–8.

6 Karl Marx, *Capital*, vol. I, trans. Ben Fowkes (London: Penguin, 1990), ch. 6.

7 *Ibid.*

8 *Ibid.*

9 See Alan Cabantous, *Histoire de la nuit: XVIIe–XVIIIe siècle* [*History of the Night: 17th–18th Century*] (Paris: Fayard, 2009) p. 140.

10 *Ibid.*, p. 141.

11 *Ibid.*, p. 143.

12 *Ibid.*, p. 146.

13 *Ibid.*

14 *Ibid.*, p. 249. See also Wolfgang Schivelbusch, *Disenchanted Night: The Industrialisation of Light in the 19th Century* (Berkeley: University of California Press,

1998); Eric le Nabour, *La Reynie, le policier de Louis XIV* [*La Reynie: Louis XIV's Policeman*] (Paris: Perrin, 1993).

15 Cabantous, *Histoire de la nuit*, p. 250.

16 Le Nabour, *La Reynie*, p. xx.

17 See Drew Durniak, 'Where Music and Passion Are Always in Fashion', *Off the Grid*, 18 July 2011, http://gvshp.org/blog/2011/07/18/where-music-and-passion-are-always-in-fashion. More generally, see Peter C. Baldwin, *In the Watches of the Night: Life in the Nocturnal City, 1820–1930* (Chicago: University of Chicago Press, 2012).

18 Schivelbusch, *Disenchanted Night*.

19 Webster Hall still served this function in 1910. Margaret Sanger, the promoter of the Pill, fed 100 strikers' children there during the workers' struggles that shook the textile sector in Lawrence, Massachusetts. See Steven Greenhouse, 'New York, Cradle of Labor History', *The New York Times*, 30 August 1996, www.nytimes/1996/08/30/arts/new-york-cradle-of-labor-history.html.

20 See Marcela Iacub, *Par un trou de la serrure: Une histoire de la pudeur publique (XIXe–XXIe siècle)* [*Through the Keyhole: A History of Public Modesty* (Paris: Fayard, 2008) p. 67.

21 Louis Chevalier, *Classes laborieuses et classes dangereuses à Paris pendant la première moitié du XIXe siècle* [*The Working Classes and the Dangerous Classes in the First Half of the Nineteenth Century*] [1958] (Paris: Perrin, 2007). On all this, read Jacques Rancière, *La nuit des prolétaires: Archive du rêve ouvrier* [*Night of*

the Proletarians: Archives of the Worker Dream] (Paris: Fayard, 1981).

22 See James A. Inciardi, 'The Changing Life of Mickey Finn: Some Notes on Chloral Hydrate down through the Ages', *Journal of Popular Culture*, 11, 3, 1977, p. 591.

23 *Ibid.*, p. 592.

24 *Ibid.*, p. 593.

25 On the 'biopolitics' of speed and MDMA, see Pascal Nouvel, *Histoire des amphetamines* [*History of Amphetamines*] (Paris: Presses universitaires de France, 2009).

26 http://en.wikipedia.org/wiki/Berghain.

27 Jonathan Crary, *24/7: Late Capitalism and the Ends of Sleep* (New York: Verso Books, 2014).

28 *Ibid.*

4 Swallowing the Pill

1 See Jonathan Eig, *The Birth of the Pill: How Four Pioneers Reinvented Sex and Launched a Revolution* (London: Pan Macmillan, 2014) p. 249.

2 *Ibid.*, p. 58.

3 *Ibid.*, p. 157.

4 *Ibid.*, p. 258.

5 Barbara Seaman, *The Doctor's Case Against the Pill* [1969], 2nd edn (Alameda: Hunter House, 1995).

6 Morton Mintz, *The Pill: The Alarming Report* (Boston: Beacon Press, 1970). On Nelson, see Bill Christofferson, *The Man from Clear Lake: Earth Day Founder Gaylord Nelson* (Madison: University of Wisconsin Press, 2004). On the 'Nelson Hearings',

see Elaine Tyler May, *America and the Pill: A History of Promise, Peril, and Liberation* (New York: Basic, 2010).

7 *Ibid.*, p. xx.

8 *Ibid.* For a commentary on this point, see Claire Gino, 'La pilule: Biologisation de la contraception et régulation sociale' ['The Pill: The Biologization of Contraception and Social Regulation'], *Genre, sexualité et société*, 12, Autumn 2014, http://gss.revues.org/3280.

9 The bibliography of the relations between Sanger and the eugenics movements in the US in the first half of the twentieth century is huge, and oscillates between hagiography and demonization. The most recent research, tending mostly towards the first, is Jean H. Baker's *Margaret Sanger, A Life of Passion* (London: Macmillan, 2011).

10 See John Henderson, *A Life of Ernest Starling* (London: Academic Press, 2005).

11 See John Henderson, 'Ernest Starling and "Hormones": An Historical Commentary', *Journal of Endocrinology*, 184, January 2005, p. 5.

12 On all this, see Holly Grigg-Spall, *Sweetening the Pill, or How We Got Hooked on Hormonal Birth Control* (Winchester, WA: Zero, 2013).

13 See Healy, *The Antidepressant Era.*

14 *Ibid.*

15 *Ibid.*

16 Charlotte Wessel Skovlund, Lina Steinrud Morch, Lars Vedel Kessing and Øjvind Lidegaard, 'Association of Hormonal Contraception with Depression', *JAMA Psychiatry*, 73, 11, 2016, p. 1154.

17 *Ibid.*, p. 1162.
18 See Holly Grigg-Spall, 'The Pill is Linked to Depression – and Doctors Can No Longer Ignore It', *Guardian*, 3 October 2016, https://www.theguardian.com/com mentisfree/2016/oct/03/pill-linked-depression-doctor s-hormonal-contraceptives.
19 *Ibid.*
20 See Grigg-Spall, *Sweetening the Pill*, p. 177.
21 Beatriz Preciado, *Testo Junkie: Sexe, drogue et biopolitique* (Paris: Grasset, 2008), trans. into English from the Spanish by Bruce Benderson as *Testo Junkie: Sex, Drugs and Biopolitics in the Pharmacopornographic Era* (New York: The Feminist Press, 2013). Page references below are from the French version [trans. note].
22 *Ibid.*, p. 138.
23 *Ibid.*, p. 23.
24 Laboria Cuboniks, 'Accélérer le féminisme', in *Accélération!*, ed. Laurent de Sutter (Paris: Presses universitaires de France, 2016) p. 253.
25 See Ewen Chardronnet, 'L'œuf, la poule et les hormones DIY', *Makery*, 18 May 2016, www.makery. info/2016/05/18/loeuf-la-poule-et-les-hormones-diy.
26 Amongst the pollutants that can be found in water, along with the hormones left over from consumption of the Pill, there are also traces of antidepressants. On this point, see Kirsten Moore, Kimberley Inez McGuire, Rivka Gordon and Tracey Woodruff, 'Birth Control Hormones in Water: Separating Myth from Fact', *Contraception*, 84, 2, 2011, p. 115.

5 The Politics of Overexcitement

1 See Olivier Bosc, *La foule criminelle: Politique et criminalité dans l'Europe du tournant du XIXe siècle* [*The Delinquent Crowd: Politics and Criminality in Europe at the Turn of the 19th Century*] (Paris: Payard, 2007).

2 *Ibid.*, p. xx. The French translation of Sighele's book appeared in 1892. The page references given below refer to the 2nd edition: Scipio Sighele, *La foule criminelle* [*The Delinquent Crowd*], trans. into French by Paul Vigny (Paris: Alcan, 1901).

3 *Ibid.*, p. 40.

4 *Ibid.*, p. 14.

5 *Ibid.*, p. 39.

6 Bosc, *La foule criminelle: Politique et criminalité.*

7 See Dominique Reynié, 'Gabriel Tarde, théoricien de l'opinion' ['Gabriel Tarde: Theorist of Opinion'] in Gabriel Tarde, *L'opinion et la foule* (Paris: Presses universitaires de France, 1989) p. 7.

8 Sighele, *La foule criminelle*, p. 156.

9 Bosc, *La foule criminelle: Politique et criminalité.*

10 Tarde, *L'opinion et la foule*, p. 49.

11 *Ibid.*

12 *Ibid.*, p. 67.

13 On the history of enthusiasm, allow me to refer to Laurent de Sutter, *Théorie du kamikaze* [*Theory of the Kamikaze*] (Paris: Presses universitaires de France, 2016) p. 45.

14 Gustave Flaubert, *L'éducation sentimentale* [*Sentimental Education*] in *Oeuvres*, ed. Réné Dumesnil and Alfred Thibaudet, vol. II (Paris: Gallimard, 1936) p. 323, cited

by Pierre Moscovici, *L'âge des foules: Un traité histo-rique de psychologie des masses* [*The Age of Crowds: A Historical Treatise of Mass Psychology*] (Paris: Fayard, 1985) p. 38.

15 Sighele, *La foule criminelle.* p. 75, n. 1.

16 *Ibid.*

17 Sigmund Freud, *Group Psychology and the Analysis of the Ego*, trans. James Strachey (New York: Boni and Liveright, 1922).

18 *Ibid.*

19 *Ibid.*

20 *Ibid.*

21 Wilhelm Reich, *The Mass Psychology of Fascism*, trans. Vincent Carfango (New York: Farrar, Straus and Giroux, 1971); José Ortega y Gasset, *The Revolt of the Masses*, trans. anon. (New York and London: W. W. Norton, 1957); Hermann Broch, *Théorie de la folie des masses* (1930–51), trans. into French by Pierre Rusch and Didier Renault (Paris and Tel Aviv: l'Eclat, 2008); Elias Canetti, *Crowds and Power* [1960], trans. Carol Stewart (London: Phoenix, 2000).

22 On the links between being and police, see the develop-ments found in Laurent de Sutter, *Poétique de la police* [*Poetics of the Police*] (Aix-en-Provence and Cologne: Rouge Profond – Klostermann, 2017).

23 Giorgio Agamben, *Opus Dei: An Archaeology of Duty*, trans. Adam Kotsko (Stanford, CA: Stanford University Press, 2013). For a commentary, see Laurent de Sutter, 'Contre Iurem: Sur les deux ontologies de Giorgio Agamben' ['Against Iurem: On the Two Ontologies of Giorgio Agamben'], forthcoming.

24 Alfred Ernout and Antoine Meillet, *Dictionnaire éty-mologique de la langue latine. Histoire des mots* [*DFHJL*], 4th edn (Paris: Klincksieck, 2001) p. 119.

25 Titus Livius, *Histoire romaine*, X, 8, 10.

26 Tarde, *L'opinion et la foule*, pp. 10, 13, 78.

27 See Luc Huffschmitt, 'Kraepelin à Java' ['Kraepelin in Java'], *Synapses*, 86, 1992, p. 69.

28 On this point, see Jodi Dean, *Crowds and Party* (London and New York: Verso, 2016), which empha-sizes the affectionate dimension at work in politics. Curiously, this is completely missing in Ernesto Laclau's extensive book *On Populist Reason* (New York: Verso, 2005).

Epilogue: Gettin' Up

1 See Susan Buck-Morss, 'Aesthetics and Anaesthetics: Walter Benjamin's Artwork Essay Reconsidered', *October*, 62, 1992.

2 *Ibid.*

3 Zimmer, *Histoire de l'anesthésie.*

4 Buck-Morss, 'Aesthetics and Anaesthetics'.